Recollections

of the late Fleet Admiral

CHESTER W. NIMITZ

as given by his widow, Catherine Freeman Nimitz

U. S. Naval Institute
Annapolis, Maryland
1970

Preface

These manuscripts are the result of several interviews with Mrs. Chester W. Nimitz, Sr. at her home in San Francisco, California. They were conducted in June, 1969 by John T. Mason, Jr., Director of the Oral History office in the U. S. Naval Institute; in March, 1970 by Professor E. B. Potter of the U. S. Naval Academy.

Only minor emendations and corrections were made by Mrs. Nimitz to the transcript. The reader is asked to bear in mind, therefore, that he is reading a transcript of the spoken word, rather than the written word.

These interviews are part of a series dealing with the late Fleet Admiral Chester W. Nimitz and were intended primarily for use in the preparation of a biography of the late Fleet Admiral.

DECLARATION OF TRUST

The undersigned does hereby appoint and designate as his (her) Trustee herein, the Secretary-Treasurer and Publisher of the United States Naval Institute to perform and discharge the following duties, powers, and privileges in connection with the possession and use of a certain taped interview between the undersigned and the Oral History Department of the United States Naval Institute.

(1) As an <u>Open</u> transcript it may be read (or the tape audited) by qualified researchers upon presentation of proper credentials as determined by the Trustee. In the case of interviews about the late Fleet Admiral C. W. Nimitz, it is intended that first use of the material shall be made by the biographer of the Fleet Admiral, Professor E. B. Potter, and the Naval Institute is authorized to deal with the material in this fashion.

(2) It is expressly understood that in giving this authorization, I am in no way precluded from placing such restrictions as I may desire upon use of the interview at any time during my lifetime, nor does this authorization in any way affect my rights to the copyright of any literary expressions that may be contained in the interview.

Witness my hand and seal this __8__ day of __June__ 19__70__

Catherine F. Nimitz

I hereby accept and consent to the foregoing Declaration of Trust and the powers therein conferred upon me as Trustee:

R. E. Bowler
Secretary-Treasurer and Publisher

Interview No. 1 with Mrs. Chester W. Nimitz
    at her apartment in San Francisco
By John T. Mason, Jr.
Date: 4 June 1969

Q: What a pleasure, Mrs. Nimitz, to see you again and what a privilege to have you talk on tape. You know, of course, that your recollections of the Fleet Admiral are going to be of tremendous value to a biographer when the family decides upon one.

Mrs. N.: Well, I assure you that my recollections are still very clear in my mind of the first time I met the Admiral. He was then a very young lieutenant. He had just passed from the rank of ensign to lieutenant, not junior grade, they had skipped the junior grade on him, so he had become a regular lieutenant. This was in 1911 and at our home in Wollaston, Massachusetts. One afternoon Lieutenant Prentice Bassett came to the front door. Lieutenant Bassett was boarding at a house just down the street from us, with his mother. He had with him on this afternoon a blond, blue-eyed gentleman named Chester Nimitz. He was bringing Chester Nimitz out to have supper with his mother, and then he said he wanted to come up and play bridge with my father and sister. My sister was much closer to Chester Nimitz' age than I was.

Q: Was that the Miss Freeman?

Mrs. N.: Yes, but Miss Freeman - my sister was not at home and so I was to play bridge with them that night. But as we

Mrs. Nimitz #1 - 2

sat there in the afternoon having a cup of tea, I who looked over at this young gentleman, whom Prentice had brought, and thought he was the handsomest person I had ever seen in my life. He had curly, blond hair, which definitely was a little bit too long because he had just come in from weeks at sea and had not had a chance to have it cut.

Q: Was he a submariner at that point?

Mrs. N.: Yes, he was in submarines at that time. And he sat there on the couch - on the sofa - behind the living room table and listened to Prentice carrying on a terrific conversation, because Prentice was always full of spirit, and he, being used to being in the house, and used to visitng with us always had something funny to say, and I kept thinking what a really lovely person this was he brought with him. Those beautiful blue eyes and a lovely smile, with which my husband greeted my mother and talked with her. They went back to the boarding house for dinner, and then came in the evening to play bridge. I was not usually chosen as a bridge partner, but because my sister was away, I did play bridge that night, and my recollection of the evening was that father and I played Prentice Bassett and Chester Nimitz. And Prentice who always carried on a sort of wild conversation and teased Lieutenant Nimitz terrifically, and it seemed to roll off of Chester's back. He didn't seem - to mind it in the slightest. We had a very pleasant evening of bridge and then they left. Then I discovered that Lieutenant Nimitz was going to assume command of the E-1, which was then

Mrs. Nimitz #1 - 3

building at the Fore River Shipbuilding Company in Quincy. He came again to call in a little while bringing with him Clarence Hinkamp, Lieutenant Clarence Hincamp, known as Heinie, Chester Nimitz was to have the E-1 and Hinkamp was to have the E-2. They went to Quincy to find a place to live, and at that time the only hotel in Quincy was the Greenleaf Hotel, which must have been built back about 1870 and was very much on its last legs. They did not serve meals there. They had perhaps one or two maids still around the joint to clean it up. They took rooms there and they ate in restaurants in Quincy. They soon began coming to the house rather regularly...

Q: Was it obvious at that point that he was interested in you?

Mrs. N.: Well, I think they were interested in having a good meal in a good home, and my mother was a marvelous cook. So that they came frequently and after a short time, they spent almost every weekend with us, the weekends starting on Friday night and ending on Tuesday morning.

Q: Oh, my.

Mrs. N.: Of course, they went to work on Monday, but they still stayed at the house. During that winter my sister and I had the most gorgeous time because the four of us went to Boston, to all the shows that came, to Keith's Vaudeville Circuit to see the different plays that were coming up at that time. We also went to bowl a great deal. We bowled in Boston, and in

Boston you bowled candlepins, the small pins.

Q: Lady pins?

Mrs. N.: Lady pins. We had a delightful time doing that. We took many, many long walks, and we had great fun at the house. And as I was always known - thought of as the young daughter, youngest daughter, nobody thought that they were being anything but very nice to me, with the result that it made it very easy for Chester and me to have a very good time together. And in 1912, during the summer of 1912, the submarines went down to Provincetown Harbor for maneuvers and trials, and so forth. By that time Lieutenant Bassett had married an old Army sweetheart of his, and they were there and had a cottage, so they invited my sister and myself to come down and spend a week there. My sister was rather dictatorial about it. She kept saying, "Catherine, don't do this. Katherine, don't do that," and I remember at dinner on the ship - that was when they still had wine in the messes...

Q: That was before Josephus Daniels.

Mrs. N.: Yes, this was before Josephus, and we had wine for dinner, and Chester and I were sitting there with some of the people at the table we were at, my sister and the others were at other tables, and my sister rushed over and said to me, "Don't take that wine. You mustn't drink any wine." And for the first time, I heard Chester Nimitz get up and say to her, "Elizabeth, I'm looking after your sister and I have no intention of letting her drink too much wine, but she's going to have a glass of wine." This was late summer. So, the following fall, about September of 1912, we became engaged and he left for a winter in Cuban waters with his new submarine, and he also had the D boats and the E boats with him. He was then in command of the Atlantic Submarine Flotilla. Lieutenant Bassett had left submarines by that time.

Q: What happned to Lieutenant Hinkamp?

Mrs. N. Lieutenant Hinkamp had the E-2, and he was in the squadron. And Lieutenant Hinkamp was a delightful, gay Dutchman. Just couldn't be nicer. So we really had a wonderful time with those youngsters. You see before Chester had shown up, I was considered so very, very young...

Q: How old were you at that point?

Mrs. N.: I was 19 when I first met him. I was considered so young that they always sort of pushed me in the background because the officers that had been used to coming to the house were the officers from the USS Vermont, and it was Commander Bertolet who was the executive, and Bill Dardy the engineer, and Harry Bringer who was the ordnance officer, and a number of others, some of them younger, some of them older. So that I rather resented naval officers because it seemed to me that my high school friends and my younger boy friends and girl friends, I couldn't have them there so often because these other people were always around. My father enjoyed playing bridge. He enjoyed having these naval officers there. My mother...

Q: What was his background, what was he?

Mrs. Nimitz #1 - 6

Mrs. N.: My father was a ship broker. He couldn't go out in a row boat without getting sick.

Q: So you found the naval officers a bit condescending?

Mrs. N.: Well, I felt that they weren't interested in me and I was interested in younger people, but when Chester Nimitz showed up, I changed my views on naval officers very definitely. He left for Cuba and we decided that we would be married as soon as we found out when he could get back, and he was getting back on I think he got in on the 8th of April, and we were married on the 9th of April 1913. After our wedding, we went on to New York and as I had only been out of Massachusetts once in my life, this was terribly exciting. We took the sleeping car on to New York.

Q: Did you have a church wedding?

Mrs. N.: No, we had a wedding in our own home. The house was decorated entirely with daffodils and my family were not very religious, but there was a Unitarian minister lived across the way from us, with great sideburns and beard and all, and he performed the marriage ceremony. The ushers were all submarine officers & my brother, excepting the best man was G. V. Stewart, a classmate of Chester's and who had been his roommate.

Q: And your maid of honor was your sister?

Mrs. N.: My maid of honor was my sister. And my brother came from Michigan for the wedding. My brother was the only one who was rather unhappy about it, and he was unhappy because he and I had been, although the difference was - he was older than my sister - the difference between us in age was six years. He was extremely fond of me and he said when he went out to Michigan in mining engineering, that as soon as I was old enough, he was going to get me to come out and keep house for him. And here I was going off and getting married.

Q: Well, that was a great loss.

Mrs. N.: That was a loss. But the wedding was a very pretty home wedding, and then we went on to New York.

Q: Was any of the Admiral's family there?

Mrs. N.: No, none of the Admiral's family were there. We went and spent a few days in New York, which was terribly exciting for me, and I must say that one of the things which Chester and I were hilarious about was that we stayed at the new Hotel McAlpin, and we were up on about the 13th or 14th floor, and on top of this building opposite - I don't remember what the building was - but there was a Wrigley's Spearmint advertisement, and all night long this girl winked her eye at us, which convulsed us both. We thought this was absolutely lovely. And I was so excited that I was standing down in the lobby and a man came up and spoke to me and I looked at him absolutely blankly and he said, "Catherine Freeman, I've lived in Wollaston near you for years."

Q: And you didn't know your next door neighbor?

Mrs. N.: I just wasn't seeing anybody but Chester, he was the only thing I could see at that time.

Q: Did you go to shows or anything?

Mrs. N.: Oh, yes, we went to shows and we window shopped because

Mrs. Nimitz #1 - 8

he had just had, I think his pay at that time was $215 a month, of which he was sending $25 home to his mother. So there wasn't much money to spend on anything very vital, but we had a wonderful time just being in New York and going about. And then we went from there down to Texas to introduce me to his family, and I think his family greeted me with mixed emotions, but I became very good friends with all of them, and we came back from there and stopped in Washington for a while.

Q: Would you digress and tell me something about the Texas welcome? You did before we went on tape.

Mrs. N.: Well, I think that they were frankly disappointed that he hadn't married a southern girl and a girl that would be living close to them so that he would always come back to Texas, because my husband had left home before he was sixteen and gone on to Bobby Werntz' school in Annapolis, and then had gone into the Naval Academy. From then on I think the longest time he ever spent in Texas was a week perhaps once in five years or something like that. So when I came down they looked a little askance at this typical Yankee that had come down, and one evening when they were all gathered around, one aunt whom I had sensed was not very fond of me looked at me dubiously - she just was sort of suspicious. She looked at me and then looked at Chester and with the assembled multitude of aunts and uncles, and as both Chester's mother and

Mrs. Nimitz #1 - 9

stepfather were each one of eleven, there were plenty of them, she said, "Chester, if there was another war between the North and the South, which would you fight with?" giving me a look that said, "now you'll see exactly where you stand." And I was very stunned, having been brought up from childhood that the Civil War was over, that it was something that you never mentioned. So for a second I sort of drew my breath in and then I looked at my husband and I'm afraid there was a very wicked twinkle in my eye, because my husband looked at them and said, "Why, I'd stay by the Union, of course." The look the aunt gave me was utterly poisonous, but we later became friends, and I think they all enjoyed having us home and seeing us, and taking a good look at me.

Q: A very difficult circumstance for a young bride far from home, wasn't it?

Mrs. N.: Definitely far from home. I think his mother, and his grandmother were darling people. Grandmother was to come over to meet me, and this I have never forgotten because it was the aftermath of a comment made by my husband to my mother before we were married. He said...My husband had been telling my mother about his mother's relatives and he said, "You know, my grandmother Henke is 96 years old and she's very wonderful." He added, "You know, I have an uncle younger than I am," and I think both Mother and I gave a quick swallow. He said, "Yes, my grandmother's youngest son is 26." Mother looked at me and we made no comment whatsoever.

Q: ~~Sarah~~.

Mrs. N.: Then I met Grandmother Heinke, who was a very stout, black-eyed little lady with a very wonderful twinkle in her eye. She spoke not very much English.

Q: She was German?

Mrs. N.: She was German. And I got her aside finally and I asked her. ~~I said,~~ "Grandmother, how old are you?" and she said, "I'm 69." Then I proceeded to tell her about her grandson's comment to my mother, and I thought Grandmother would die laughing. And all the afternoon, she would suddenly look around the room and she'd look at Chester, then she'd look at me, and she would go into shrieks of laughter, and her family all wondered what ailed her.

Q: He was just a bit confused.

Mrs. N.: He was more than confused. Well now, I think that from there - then we went back to New York and I will start that later on.

Interview #2 with Mrs. Chester W. Nimitz

By John T. Mason, Jr.

Date 5 June 1969

Q: Now, Mrs. Nimitz, ~~today~~ this is interview No. 2 on the 5th of June. Do you want to continue by saying something more about the Texas family?

Mrs. N. Yes. My husband loved to tell about his grandfather Nimitz taking him off during vacations on fishing trips. Grandfather would take a big old Prarie schooner with horses, and tell Chester he could invite a guest, and so Chester would take some other little boy with him. They would go off for, perhaps, a week at a time. Grandfather would keep camp and would do all the cooking.

Q: This is Grandfather Heinke?

Mrs. N.: No, this is Grandfather Nimitz. And Grandfather Nimitz would do all the cooking and the camp keeping and the little boys fished to their hearts' content or hunted in the woods. And Chester always said that was one of the pleasantest memories of his childhood, these trips with his grandfather. He also enjoyed very, very much going out to the farm, the Heinke farm, to his Grandfather Heinke's where he had all kinds of wonderful food and was allowed to go out on the range with the cowboys. But I think the most delightful story of all of his childhood is the one that my husband always shook his head over and said, "How could he have done it?" On the first day that Chester was to go to school, and he had spoken

German most of his life and had been rather separated from children in some ways, he went to school, and his Grandfather Nimitz for some unaccountable reason insisted on giving him a small Derby hat to wear to school. Chester went rather timidly anyhow and as he got into the schoolyard, he hadn't got two feet in before someone knocked off the hat. Well, Chester immediately went and got the hat, put it on again, and someone else knocked it off. Well, before he ever got in the school, the hat was demolished. Chester's eyes were more or less black and his clothes were torn. But he fought all that day because of that hat. And for years afterwards, in fact, the last few months before he died he said to me, "Why, why do you suppose Grandfather ever gave me that hat to wear to school?"

Q: That's an unanswered question.

Mrs. N.: Here he was bare-footed with just a pair of jeans and a shirt on, with a Derby hat.

Q: Was this in Kerrville?

Mrs. N.: This was in Fredericksburg. I think that this was one of the unanswered problems of the Admiral's life as to why his grandfather did this, what had he meant to do? And another one of the experiences that the Admiral had as a small boy: he had two girl cousins that were nearer his age than most of the other nieces and nephews and grandchildren, and one of these girls and Chester were playing together - they were very young - and they had some pinwheels and rockets. This was just about the 4th of July, and Chester didn't know how to work this rocket, but he and this young cousin were in a bedroom in his grandfather's hotel, and they decided to see if they could light the rocket. Well, they did, and it started off at a mad pace going up and hitting the ceiling and going across and hitting a wall, down to the floor, and they both got so scared that they got under the corner of the bed as far up as they could get, because occasionally the rocket went under the bed. And Chester said he was taught then not to meddle with what you didn't know about. The room was a shambles.

Q: He learned a lot of little lessons like that, didn't he?

Mrs. N.: He certainly did. I think Chester was like his son, very experimental and very anxious to find out why things did what they did. I remember when we were visiting Grandmother Nimitz on our way out to Honolulu, young Chester Jr. was playing in the back yard of Grandmother's house and there was an old Negro woman who was doing the laundry for Grandmother, and all of a sudden she heard a shriek from Chester. She looked over, and here was this little five-year old boy literally covered with bees, and she called her son and they grabbed him, and they probably saved his life because they took him in and immediately poured blueing all over him, just slopped it on everywhere. They said his hands were full of bees, his eyes, his head, everything, he had over 40 or 50 stings. They got the child finally quieted and got the bees off of him, and when we got home, we had been out visiting another relative, when we got home that night,

Mrs. Nimitz #2 - 14

Chester was sitting up in bed, not so badly swollen as you would have expected, because this blueing is the one thing that would have knocked the bee stings out.

Q: How did she know that? Is it...?

Mrs. N.: As instinct, and the fact that apparently it was an old remedy that they had known for years.

Q: A chemical reaction.

Mrs. N.: Yes, what is it that blueing has in it? It's some substance in blueing that absolutely knocks the bee stings out. But as we went in to see our swollen, subdued son, he just looked at us and said, "But how do they get the honey out of the hives?"

Q: Not this way, certainly.

Mrs. N.: And so whenever Chester, young Chester made any comments that we thought were a little bit - that he was wondering about something, we'd say, "Well, Chester, how do they get the honey out of the hives?" Be careful. Now, let me see if there were any other stories to tell about. No, excepting the Admiral used to say that the boys he played with in Kerrville when he was older and going to high school were very - they were the sons of the bankers, presidents of banks, and the president of the big store in Kerrville, and Chester said that whatever they did they always got out of it and he was always blamed for everything. I think that possibly some of the blame probably belonged on him because he had a certain amount of deviltry in him, but he later became very close friends with all these people, and they were the

Mrs. Nimitz #2 - 15

first to honor him when he came back at the end of the war. But they had very exciting times there. He used to go fishing and hunting, and he loved to spend much time with the Army people that came down there in the summer for their summer encampment, regular Army officers, West Pointers.

Q: They stayed at the hotel, didn't they?

Mrs. N.: Yes, well some of them. No, their camp was just outside and they would come in to the hotel for meals, but he would meet them and he'd talk with these people and it was through them that he realized that his only chance for getting an education was to get an appointment, as he thought, to West Point. And when the West Point appointments were all filled, then he had to take Annapolis. And it's rather interesting to note that Eisenhower wanted to go to the Naval Academy and couldn't get an appointment to the Naval Academy, so he took one at West Point. Thus do fortunes change.

Q: I've run into any number of naval officers who wanted to go to West Point and there was no appointment.

Mrs. N.: Well, now let me see. What should we do after this?

Q: Would you tell me the story, as you understand it, of his rescue of the fireman?

Mrs. N.: Of the fireman?

Q: This was before you were married?

Mrs. N.: Yes, but he was writing to me every day and I got a letter and all it said was, "I had to go swimming yesterday and it was awfully, awfully cold." Because it was winter, late fall, in Chesapeake Bay. Then I got a letter from an other man who Heine Hinkamp used to be at the house a great deal with Chester, and he told me about Chester's rescuing this man. Now, later on, after we were married, Chester told the whole thing. He was on his ship, on the mother ship, and he saw a fireman fall over, and the current was terrifically strong there.

Q: This was in the Bay?

Mrs. N.: Yes. In Hampton Roads. And he realized that the man could not swim. So Chester went after him. He had to fight the man as well as the sea, and when - he kept the man's head above water, but he realized that they were going out to sea, and he couldn't get back against this current lugging this man, and a boat from another ship - I think it was, I don't remember, but it seems to me the <u>North Dakota</u> strikes my mind, (but it was from one of the battleships) came over and pulled them both out of the water. But although he had been in the water a long time with this man, I don't think it did Chester any harm. He seemed to be in perfectly good health. I think they kept him wrapped up for a few hours and gave them care.

Q: But his remark to you was that he simply had to go swimming?

Mrs. N.: Yes, he went swimming and said, "I went swimming yesterday and - it was very cold," and that was all he said to me in his letter.

Q: You say he wrote you every day during...

Mrs. N.: Every day

Q: ...the courtship?

Mrs. Nimitz #2 - 17

Mrs. N.: He wrote me every day during the Second World War.

Q: He did, indeed?

Mrs. N.: We always wrote each other every day. If we missed it was a very rare thing, some of them were short, but it just sort of was a safety valve for him to do this.

Q: How remarkable.

Mrs. N.: I remember Allan Nevins said, "Have you any of your husband's letters?" I said, "No, I burned them."

Q: Did you really?

Mrs. N.: Yes, I burned almost every one of them. In fact, I thought I'd burned them all, and then I found that there were a few that I had missed. They were in another box. But I still say that no one should read those letters because a man talks to his wife. She's a safety valve. Allan Nevins was quite disgusted when I said to him, "Look, a man has to have some safety valve." Now, I did go through some of the letters and take out excerpts just that were telling about his going out walking in the afternoon and doing this, that, and the other. But that was all. And I admit the few that I found I kept. I have one letter which I will show you which is the letter he wrote me after he had signed the Japanese terms.

Q: Oh, I'm glad you saved that one.

Mrs. N.: Yes. I've always saved that. That's been in the safe deposit box. Then I took it out because it was written on the paper that they *used as programs on V.J. signing day* I took it out of the safe deposit box and brought it home. I brought it home because it was getting cracked you see..

Interval

Q: Um, that's signed in the correct place, isn't it?

Mrs. N.: Yes.

Q: Would you want to read this into the tape?

Mrs. N.: I will.

Q: All right, Would you?

This is the letter of Admiral Nimitz to his wife after the signing in Tokyo Bay:

Mrs. N.: USS South Dakota, Tokyo Bay, Sunday, 2nd of September '45

Best beloved, The big moment is over and the Japs have signed the formal terms of surrender. Everything clicked in a minute by minute schedule and the ceremony started at exactly 9 a.m. Tokyo time. The press came off in a transport destroyer before 8 a.m. followed by another destroyer carrying

Mrs. Nimitz #2 - 19

all the guests except the Supreme Commander's private party, which came alongside as did all the destroyers at 8.30. I don't see how I can describe this scene, or why I attempt it, because there were present at least 200 correspondents who have by now written, and broadcast thousands of words of decription which, even as I write at 11.30 a.m., is either being read or heard by you and all our children wherever they may be. Many of our officers from the ships still at sea were present, they having flown in by plane. Among those was Shaffroth who particularly asked that I include in this letter my (R) best wishes to you and Mary. Fortunately the bad weather for the past two days passed on and we were blessed with dry, though overcast, skies. Last night I was tremendously pleased and surprised to receive your fine letters of the 23rd and the 24th of August with the enclosures which were brought up from Guam by one of our officers who brought up important mail. This is rapid time for your 24th of August letter written on my 25th with only seven days from Berkeley to Tokyo Bay. Now I must close. All my heart's devotion. Love and kisses to my sweetheart. Ever yours, Chester.

On the back of the letter is written:

Every Turret top, every point of vantage was occupied by newsmen, cameramen, including local Japanese papers and officers and men from the ship who could get a foothold. When it came time to sign, I confess to nervous excitement but I did sign in the correct places. One signer did not. First

Mrs. Nimitz #2 - 20

copy signed with the Wo gold gift pen, and the second copy signed with my old green Parker pen.

The pen which he called the Wo pen was given him by our friends, Eching and Y. C. Wo, great friends of ours. And the other pen was a fifty-cent Parker pen that he bought from a bumboat man in our travels. That is now in the Naval Academy Museum.

Q: Oh, is it?

Mrs. N.: Yes, and it was delivered to the Naval Academy by some girls from the Dominican Convent where our daughter teaches.. When they went there they were having a trip around the East escorted by one nun and by one lay woman. The Admiral said if they were going (because he had arranged for them to visit with President Kennedy and to visit other famous people,) he said to them, "Now, I'm going to give you this most valuable pen, which you are to deliver to the Commandant of the Naval Academy. And there's a delightful picture taken when the girls got to Washington to see President Kennedy, it was his birthday and he took them right into his private office all these, oh, they were utterly charming looking girls and they were all very pretty wearing the uniform of the school, one girl showed him the pen, and I think when he took it in his hands she said, "But you can't have it." He said, no, he understood that. He could just look at it. This was something that they had to deliver to the Naval Academy and they delivered it and saw the Naval Academy, and went to a tea dance, and had a most delightful time.

Q: And it's in the Museum, right?

Mrs. N.: It's in the Museum.

Q: Right underneath my office.

Mrs. N.: Yes. Is it? This is a very wonderful letter and I like to keep it. You see - my problem is if I put it between glass, it will fade, and I can't put it between plastic because they catch on. So I'm keeping it in this most useful book of the Sierras.

Q: There is some way of treating documents now, I think. Spraying them or something. Yes, some museum person could tell you just what they do. But they do protect them adequately.

Mrs. N.: They must have to do something.

Q: I'm glad you saved that one, and you did cull through the others?

Mrs. N.: I culled through the others, but Chester and I always felt that the letters that we wrote each other were for each other, and he destroyed mine, I destroyed a good many - most of his. Otherwise, as you could imagine if we hadn't destroyed our letters there'd be no room in the house for them. Not writing every day. But let me see...

Q: Well, I got you off on a side track, talking about the swimming incident at Hampton Roads. But you were going to return to New York.

Mrs. N.: We returned to Washington from Texas on our honeymoon, and from there we went up to New London.

Mrs. Nimitz #2 - 22

From Texas we went first to Washington for a few days and then were ordered up to New London to the submarine base for the time that we were to wait before going to Europe. We went up to New London I would say in April and we went to Europe in May.

Q: This was on that diesel engine matter?

Mrs. N.: This was on the problem of the diesel engine - the big diesel engine. And of course the small diesel engines were in submarines and around the shipyard there, so we had a chance to - Chester did - to view the submarine ones.

Q: This was something he was very anxious to do, wasn't it?

Mrs. N.: Well, I think he was. He had some offers and he asked me which one I wanted to do, and he said one was to go to Newport for something, to spend our first two years in Newport. And I said, well, why don't we go to Europe first and go back to Newport later. And he remarked, "Well, darling, they won't do that because they're two different jobs. I can't have them both." But we went over on the <u>Kaiserine Augusta</u>, a beautiful ship, to Hamburg, and at Hamburg we settled down in the Outer Alster of Hamburg - at the Outer Alster of Hamburg - by it, I should say, because that being water. There was a pension where we had two rooms overlooking a lovely garden. Chester immediately started work at the Blohm and Voss works where they were building engines of that same type, not as large but where the plans for those engines had come from, you see.

Q: What was his actual mission?

Mrs. N.: He was to go over to study diesel engines because the Blohm and Voss people in Hamburg were the ones who had made the plans and therefore had all the working drawings and were building similar engines, but smaller. He was very busy, he went to work, he'd leave the house by 7.30 in the morning, and he'd get home around 7 at night. So I wandered around Hamburg and watched the lake and the boating parties that were out on it - people always boating - and what delighted both Chester and myself was the people that lived just at the edge of the Alster, as we were living, and they would come home from work, change from their business suits into Lederhosen hose, you know, and go over with a creel on their back and stand on the concrete sidewalk, put their poles over the side, put their line over the side, and fish. And catch fish, but it looked so very funny to see these people coming home and just to walk across the street to fish to get into this very elegant fishing costume.

Q: Abercrombie and Fitch.

Mrs. N.: Several very interesting incidents happened. You see, I should tell you that when we went over, the Admiral had with him a man named Kläppenberg and a man named Delbose. Kläppenberg was a draftsman and Delbose was an engineer, in the they were civilian employees for the New York Navy Yard.

Q: Oh, I see. Did they speak German?

Mrs. N.: Kläppenberg could, and Chester could speak German.

Q: Was that a factor in his appointment to do this?

Mrs. N.: No, I don't think so. He didn't speak good enough

German to have it a factor. They would go out among the shops at the Blohm and Voss works. But at that particular time, the cruiser <u>Derflinger</u> - the German cruiser <u>Derflinger</u> - was on the ways and they were going to have a terrific time when the launching came. The Kaiser was coming, all the big V.I.P,s were coming, it was going to be a terrific thing. Well, of course, Chester and his men were not invited to the launching but they could stand in the back. But, alas, all the props were knocked out and nothing happened, and there was just a <u>terrible</u> <u>consternation</u>! Nothing would start that ship down the ways. So the Kaiser returned home, everybody returned home, and Chester and his men immediately left the yard before they all came out because they knew that the Germans would be ready to murder him if they saw him there because they were so disgusted over this thing. Well, later on the <u>Derflinger</u> did finally consent to go down the ways, but she was a hard luck ship all through the war - I mean at the beginning of the war. She was sunk down off the coast of South America quite early in the war. She was a bad luck ship, and when the second launching came I think either Chester wasn't around or they told him to stay out of the yard.

Q: You were there just prior to the outbreak of the war, weren't you?

Mrs. N.: We were just prior to the outbreak. We were there in the summer of 1913 and the war started just after we came back, and we found that the Germans were very arrogant and very difficult at that time. If I were walking along the street alone and two or three German officers were coming abreast, I would have to go into the street. They would not move out for me. We both found that they were arrogant - you could see that something was going to happen. Of course, we met some utterly delightful people. Mr. Nonnenbruch - I can't remember the other man's name, the head man. And then we met a delightful banker named Brüdemann. The Brüdemann's were delightful to us, but the German people themselves were the height of arrogance at that time. We were in Hamburg for quite a long time and one very interesting thing happened while we were there. Chester and I were out on our balcony, this was on a Saturday afternoon, and all of a sudden there was a pounding on our door. Chester went in, and it was our two men who were over there with us, and they said, "Come quick, come quick. A Zeppelin has had to land on the lake." So we went out and exactly in front of our house was the Zeppelin. We had the most marvelous look at it and, oh, of course, all of Hamburg was down there in just nothing flat looking at this. Well, they worked on the engines for some time and then she rose gracefully up and took off again.

Q: Was your husband interested in lighter-than-air craft?

Mrs. N.: No. We went from Hamburg to Augsburg, and at Augsburg we stayed in the hotel that Napoleon had stayed in when he was there, when he was going marching through all Germany. We even had the same room that Napoleon had. It was an enormous room, bigger than this whole apartment, and they finally decided to cut off one corner of it, and that was a <u>big</u> corner, and make a bathroom out of it, but the bathroom wall only went up just above where you could look over, so all the sounds were audible, in the room. We stayed there for several days, and Chester was busy all day long, so I just prowled around the town by myself. But the only other person in that hotel, so far as we could make out, while we were there was a boy of Dutch citizenship but a Scotchman whose father took out his Dutch citizenship because he was building ships in Holland, and this boy was in Germany on business and he was so glad to see us, so the three of us used to spend the evenings pitching pennies in this lovely old courtyard that was in this hotel. And he gave Chester some very excellent advice, although perhaps Chester didn't need it because he wouldn't have done it anyhow, but he said, "they will sooner or later offer you plans." He said, "don't buy them." He said that's what they're waiting to catch. He said, "I've seen so many..."

Q: Offered plans? Building plans?

Mrs. N.: Building plans of something or other, some ship or something. And he said, "They're a tricky lot. I'm very careful never to have anything to do with these people when they come up and offer things. It's just a trap to catch you." Well, we had wonderful food in this hotel and Chester said to me, "How do you suppose it ever keeps going?" Because there were just the three of us there in this enormous hotel. Then from there we went to Nuremberg, and at Nuremberg

Nürnberg   Nürnberg

we stayed first at the Rotahahn. His German aunt had suggested that we go there and it was a lovely hotel. So we took a room up on the second or third floor, and then Chester said to the bell boy, "We would like to take baths. Where are the bathrooms?" And the boy said, "Get in your bath robes and then I will take you to the bathroom." So we each got into our bath robes, which fortunately were rather voluminous and covered us very well. And the next thing we discovered, we were being walked down to the lobby of the hotel, past all of the guests, to two bathrooms down there. Well Chester said, "This may be a very nice hotel, but we're not staying here any longer than we can help." So we went around and we finally found the Grand Hotel which, of course, to the Germans was too foreign a type hotel. They didn't like it. But by taking a room up under the eaves we also could get a bath attached to it. So we took that.

Q: American style.

Mrs. N.: American style, and we went there to live. The Admiral worked very hard but we have some very lovely memories of that stay in Nurnberg, because there was a charming gentleman there connected with the Augsburg and Nurnberg Machinen Fabric, an engineering plant, who took us to the Frankeschwitz on a Sunday in a great big car. And we went up all these lovely mountain roads and it was a period when poppies, big red poppies, and blue cornflowers were just massed in all of the fields. It was absolutely gorgeous with these white-crowned mountains behind. We had the most lovely day took us to lunch in a mountain inn, where we saw the trout being caught, that we were going to eat for lunch, and they were delicious. I remember on the way back to Nüremberg that we had a very delightful episode, when a flock of geese saw us coming and immediately took right to the road and simply blocked us. You couldn't have gotten past, and there they stood hissing at us, and finally their goose girl caught up with them and began belaying them with her stick, and finally got these geese so that we could get by. We couldn't make a move.

Q: They didn't like Americans, either.

Mrs. N.: They didn't like Americans, either. So when we stayed at the gravel hotel we got a great deal of pleasure. We would sit downstairs at night and watch - some of the German generals that were there with their wives. Their wives were terrifically plump, husky women, and to see these very stout generals and their stout wives sitting there in the evening drinking Napoleon brandy out of great big snifters, and at the bottom would be just a few drops of Napoleon brandy, and they would sniff it, and sniff it, and sniff it, and then they would twirl it around, and then they would take a little sip. And Chester and I would sit behind the palms so they couldn't see us and get such a kick out of watching this proceeding, because they were just as arrogant as they could be. We just got pushed around terrifically if any of the military were there. I didn't go out very much during the day because I looked even younger than I was, and I found that when I first went out - these Germans would gather around me. If I was looking in a store window, I'd turn, and there'd be a semicircle of men around me saying, "Well, she's young. She's awfully young. Yes, but she wears a wedding ring." And then they would make comments. So I finally said I'm not going out any more, and then the American Consul said, "Oh, don't be foolish. I'll tell you just how you can get rid of them in no time." I said, "How?" He said, "Well, you know those awful shoes the Germans wear?" And I said, "Yes." So he said, "Well, people make so much fun of them that they are really sensitive. Just look at their feet and start to laugh." The next time I went down we had suddenly decided we must have something to take back with us from Germany. So I bought six little Dresden china after-dinner coffee cups. I went down to buy those cups, and I was looking in the window because there were some of them in the window, when men came and clustered all around me and began their usual comments. So I looked down at their feet, and then I pointed at their shoes and burst out laughing. I've never seen people melt out of sight as those men did. They just disappeared. From then on, I had no difficulty.

Q: That's a delightful story.

Mrs. N.: We went over to Belgium for a short time to Bruges, to a, well, some sort of a world fair that they were having there, at which some of these engines such as Chester was going to build were on the rack.

Q: It was a trade fair?

Mrs. N.: Yes, a trade fair. And while he looked at engines, I looked at the beautiful laces that were being made. With their thrifty ideas, they had cut each one of the bedrooms in their hotel into two, ~~see,~~ so as to make money from both of these sections. And the rooms were so small that our small trunk we had and our suitcases could not get into the room with us. We had to hire two rooms, one for the trunk and a suitcase, and one for us. We made one short trip from - oh, what is the North German port farther out towards the sea than - Bremen. We made one trip from ~~Bremen~~ Kiel to Copenhagen for a weekend and stayed at a delightful hotel. We went across the strait to Sweden and had luncheon in Sweden and were terribly amused when we were waited on by a Filipino boy, who had started out on a ship and had sailed for a while and so forth and so on, and then had decided to stop there in Sweden and wait at this hotel. We saw the place where Hamlet was supposed to be buried, and we thought Copenhagen and the Danish country very beautiful ~~and just lovel~~y. From there, we came back to Hamburg and I think we took off from Hamburg again on another ship, I don't remember - oh, it was a smaller ship, and I was - er, at that time I had discovered that we were going to have an addition to the family and I was sick as a dog coming home on the ship. So I spent most of the time lying down.

Q: This whole experience was one of the very, very happy ones in your husband's life, wasn't it?

Mrs. Nimitz #2 - 31

Mrs. N.: Yes. I think he enjoyed it very much.

Q: He talks about it in that way.

Mrs. N.: Yes, we did, we had a very entertaining time over there and I think he enjoyed the work that he was doing tremendously. I think that from there we came back to Brooklyn...

Q: I recall seeing a letter that I think he wrote his mother from abroad.

Mrs. N.: Yes, yes, he did. He wrote his mother several letters. I think now, Brooklyn was - we lived on 415 Washington Avenue in an apartment, and when I think of it now, that apartment had three really charming bedrooms, a bath, a dining room - (full sized dining room) and kitchen, and living room. A lovely living room. We paid $50 a month for it. Unfurnished, of course, we furnished it ourselves. We had a very amusing time because as soon as the submarines arrived in New York, all the men whom we had known, all the young officers whom we had known before we were married decided that they'd spend every Sunday with us, and so they would start calling early in the morning, saying "I'll be out for lunch today."

Q: That was their decision, not yours?

Mrs. N.: It was their decision, but we loved having them come. But when I think we used to - we had only $215 a month and we sent $25 home to his mother, when I think that we used to go down to the market and buy a a whole fore shoulder of lamb, boned and rolled, for 90 cents, and that was what we served every Sunday because it was the least expensive meat. We would simmer it for a certain length of time, it was highly seasoned, then we would take it out just before the end, when it was tender, put it in a baking pan, and put currant jelly over it, and then bake it till it was nice and brown. And these men just dearly loved it.

Q: No wonder they came back every week.

Mrs. N.: They came back every week.

Q: Did you do all this work yourself?

Mrs. N.: Well, I did all the cooking at that time. Towards the end we had a maid who did some of it, helped a little. But I remember one day that - these people would come early and just be there, so we would make them take off their coats and get busy. They would have to help with peeling the potatoes and fixing things. And one day Chester was taking the lamb out of the kettle in which it had been simmering and he got it out from the kettle and he dropped it on the floor. I was a little horrified because - all our guests were watching, and he with his usual calmness, stabbed it with a fork, picked it up, put it under the faucet and washed it off and said, "Just a lamb gambol," and put it in the pan and baked it. I assure you everybody ate it. We moved from Washington Avenue after Catherine was born, and moved out to Flatbush - We had two children, you see, and there wasn't a year between them, so we used to go out in the park on Sunday like all other Flatbush parents with a carriage filled with

Mrs. Nimitz #2 - 33

bottles, and pushing one child in a go-cart and pulling the other one - the fathers would be feeding the babies their bottles, taking them and running around, and most of the mothers were home cooking the dinner. When Chester found he could handle both the baby carriage in front of him and the push-cart behind him, then I stayed home and I'd have the dinner ready for them when they came back. But there was a lovely area in the park where they had busts of all the great musicians, Handel, Haydn, Mozart, and so many of these people in Flatbush were Germans and Jewish people who were greatly devoted to music, and they would take the babies out in that area, and Chester would sit there with his two babies, giving one a bottle and one a cracker during the morning, and then all the fathers would come home at noon bringing their offspring, and getting a good meal when they got there. I think that we had a great deal of fun out of our children and out of living there, and from there he went off on the <u>Maumee</u>. He went to sea, and I moved over - oh, I stayed there until - no, something happened at that time. In 1915 the <u>Lusitania</u> sank, the 7th of May, and my brother was on it, and my mother had a terrible heart attack, so I took the two children and went up to stay with her. So, at the end, when Chester went to sea, I was up in Massachusetts at the time. And later on I went back to Brooklyn, when he came in and we took another apartment.

Q: Was this the time he had the accident with his finger?

Mrs. Nimitz #2 - 34

Mrs. N.: Yes, he had the accident to his finger - it must have been when we were living in a small boarding house down nearer the Navy Yard. I must have come back from being in Wollaston for a while. Anyway, he was having a meeting of many engineers from all over the country to see these diesel engines, and he was in his nice white uniform and with clean white gloves on when one of the visiting engineers said, "How can you tell whether the exhaust in clean or not?" And he said, "Well, you can see that place in there," and he pointed. He didn't realize that these canvas gloves were about an inch beyond his finger, and the plug caught them - the only thing that saved his hand was his class ring. He had time to pull his hand back and save the rest of his hand.

Q: To save his naval career, too.

Mrs. N.: Yes, but he was very funny about it. He went up to the Naval Hospital. The first thing that happened was a young sailor who was very fond of him picked up the glove and the rest of his finger fell out, and the sailor just keeled over. That was too much for him. Chester went up to the Naval Hospital and, of course, they cleaned this stump of finger off and sewed it up without giving him any anesthetic because the hand was absolutely numb. He couldn't feel anything. After it was all finished he said, "Thank you. Now I'll go back as I have a great many guests." And the doctor said, "Now, wait, wait. Don't be hasty." And Chester said, "But

I've got a lot of guests back there." So, they said, "I tell you what. You go into this room," taking him into one of the hospital rooms, "and you stay here, and if at the end of an hour you still want to go back, we'll see about it." Well, Chester said by the end of an hour he didn't want anybody anywhere near him. That hand was hurting him so terribly. So they put him to bed. When I called the ship - Chester and I were going to make a date to do something later on in the day - and asked if I could speak to Captain Nimitz - Commander Nimitz, he was then. This voice said, "Oh, no, he's just been terribly hurt. He's in the naval hospital." I'm not a person who gets upset over news too easily, and I said, "Well, now, just a minute. Let me speak to the executive officer." So the executive officer came, and I said,(no, not the executive officer, it was the engineering officer) "What's happened to my husband?" And he said, "He's had his finger cut off. He's going to be all right. He's up at the naval hospital. But how did you know?" He said, "We have had people stationed at every single one of the phones and under no conditions - when you called were they to say anything to you." "You're a little too late," I said, "one of them forgot it." Chester got through very well and went off on the ship on its shakedown. He enjoyed very much, that ship, and as long as he was there to handle the engines-the ship had a tremendous career, but two or three years later when the original people who worked the ship and knew how to work these engines,

Mrs. Nimitz #2 - 36

left, the engines didn't do so well. They found that one had to know diesel engines.

Q: Did he pass on his know-how learnt in Germany?

Mrs. N.: Yes, he tried to pass on all of it, but when you put in a whole new bunch into a ship that have never handled those kind of engines, they just didn't do it as well. He had long since left. There are certain things about diesel engines that you have to be very careful of. Now the old Maumee is over in Taiwan as part of the fleet over there. I believe the United States gave it to China, and that brought on a delightful correspondence between Admiral Nimitz and Admiral Chow-Fei of the Chinese Navy. Because Chow-Fei was given command of this ship...

Q: How do you spell his name?

Mrs. N.: C-h-o-u and the other one is F-e-i. That brought on a correspondence between the two and then Chou-Fei was given the head of the new Naval Academy in Taiwan, and he wrote and asked the Admiral if he would send them something to inspire midshipmen to put up on their bronze doors going into the Academy. And he did, but I have not got what he said - that's known to Naval History Department in Washington, I'm sure.

Q: What was it, an inscription?

Mrs. N.: Yes, an inscription to go on it. It was a very nice inscription...

Q: Is it something that he composed?

Mrs. N.: Yes, I think so. Admiral Chou-Fei always used to send the Admiral things, among them were these vases.

Mrs. Nimitz #2 - 37

Q: You were going to tell me, Mrs. Nimitz, about what you did during the war.

Mrs. N.: Yes, well, before the war started, and I think Chester could see that there were signs coming up. I could see in his mind that while he never spoke of war, that he knew it was coming, and he had said once, "I tell you one thing, if there's another war, there is not going to be another group like the Yeomanettes, because," he said, "I don't think they're any help - I don't think they were much help." So, nothing more was said about it, but after he had gone out to Pearl Harbor and had taken over and had been out there about eight or nine months, I decided to move to California because I wanted to be out of Washington. I didn't like all the rumors that were running round, all the strange people that were running round there. You didn't know who they were or what they might be saying or listening to. So I decided to leave and come to the West Coast, and I hadn't been out there very long when I received word from Admiral Jacobs who had taken Chester's place as Chief of Navigation, asking me if I would please go on the air and broadcast to try to urge women to come into the Navy as WAVES.

W: Was this the WAVES?

Mrs. N.: This was the WAVES. They were just starting the WAVES, and Miss McAfee had come out to the West Coast as they wanted to get recruits, so Mrs. Nimitz went on the air across the continent and out into Hawaii and broadcast trying to instill a longing for the Navy into these ladies.

Q: What did your husband feel?

Mrs. N.: The funny thing is I think my husband must have been very much surprised...

Q: You didn't consult him?

Mrs. N.: No, I didn't consult him at all. Why do I have to consult him about this? The ladies had decided they wanted it, and it wasn't any of his business. They weren't going to be out with him. They were going to be in the States, and so if the Navy wanted them, I would help them. And so this broadcast went forth. I got many nice telegrams from people in the States about it, but I was highly amused over this because I thought how surprised my husband would be when he reads in the paper that his wife had been broadcasting for ladies in the Navy. And a propos of that, I must tell a delightful story; I think it was General Vandergrift told my husband and myself at the end of the war when we were having dinner with him. If any of you have been in the house of the Commandant of Marines in Washington, you know that somewhere back in the dim dark ages, some Commandant decided it would be very nice to put his portrait in the house and have all succeeding commandants painted and put in the house. Well, I don't know how you would feel, but as far as I'm concerned to take over a house, to live in, with all the former occupants of that house staring at you would be pretty bad. And I had remarked on it several times when we had been at parties at the place, that I thought this was a diabolical idea, and I certainly wouldn't agree with it. Among these portraits was a man who must have been in power around, perhaps, 1870, I would say. He had sideburns and muttonchop whiskers, and he was the most stern, forbidding-looking creature you could imagine. At the end of the war, when we were having dinner with the Vandergrifts, General Vandergrift told me this most delightful story. At the beginning of the war, when he was there with his wife they were having dinner alone, the war had been declared and he was terribly busy, he'd come home at night and there were no parties, he was exhausted. He was sitting in the dining room with his wife having dinner, and this same muttonchopped gentleman - it was an enormous portrait, it must have been about 7 feet high and about 5 feet wide - was standing there in his full glory at the side, and General Vandergrift turned to his wife and said, "Today we made history in the Marine Corps," and she said, "What do you mean?" "Well," he said, "we have finally decided to have women in the Marine Corps." With that there was this terrible crash! The portrait fell off the wall, the frame went into smithereens, and the portrait sort of shriveled up on the floor. And, he said, "I just looked up to the boys and said, 'Just take him out'". I think that's very much as it happened. I can't put the exact words in it, but I always loved it because this was my idea of that man, too. I would have swept him out long before.

Q: How much did you do in recruiting work for the Waves?

Mrs. N.: That was the only thing I did because I was at the hospital all the time. I just did the broadcast for them, and

I had a Wave as my assistant during the war. I think the Waves in the United States worked very well. There were the inevitable problems that come up under those circumstances, and Chester was very wise to say that none of them should come out to the Pacific. He didn't let them come out until the very end of the war, because he couldn't afford to have people worrying over the kind of problems that we had to worry about in the States. I think that the Waves that are in there now are a very fine bunch of women, wonderful, and they were then. Look who you had - you had Miss McAfee, you had Tovah Peterson Wiley, who is out here, she had been an executive at the Emporium for years, and she made a wonderful No. 2. on the Waves Organization.

Q: Did you know Jean Palmer?

Mrs. N.: Yes, Jean Palmer. And Mrs. Hancock, Joy Hancock, was a Wave. So many of the Waves were very dear friends of mine. And especially Frances Rich, who is now a very famous sculptor, and she's the daughter of Irene Rich, the actress.

Q: Where is she - on the West Coast?

Mrs. N.: She's here. I mean to say she's down in the San Bernadino mountains. She lives up there. Her mother has a wonderful ranch up there, and they live up there together and Frances has just had a show which was simply magnificent. Chester and I used to stop by when they lived in Santa Barbara. We used to stop by and always had dinner or lunch or some refreshments when we were going down to San Diego to see our children.

Mrs. Nimitz #2 - 41

Q: Now, a continuation of what you did during the war.

Mrs. N.: Well, I was out at the hospital - at the naval hospital - in Oakland, lovingly called Oak Knoll, from about October of '42 to the end of the war. I went out there at the request of the commanding officer who was going to open the first family hospital in the Navy, and as he and I had discussed it many times duirng my convalescence from a leg operation, he said he would like me to come out there and see if I could help them get started becaue most of the doctors in this hospital - operation - out there were to be reserve doctors and not used to Navy ways. So he put a Navy nurse who had been in the service almost 20 years and myself out in the clinic to sort of get this thing started. I remember that the day that we were to open the clinic, we discovered to our horror that all the baby clothes that the Navy had ordered for the obstetrical ward had not arrived - nothing had arrived - but there were seven babies, four or five babies due within the next 24 hours. In fact, they were coming so fast that the doctors said,, "What are we going to do?" And the Navy Relief, with its usual ability, promptly - I called them and asked them to send me a number of layettes immediately, by automobile, get them over there as fast as they could. They were gotten there in time, they were sterilized, and when the first baby arrived there was something to put her into. The babies arrived, it seemed to me, with fair regularity from then on to the end of the war. We had a great many times when the wounded came in were very sad. You would see these terribly wounded boys coming in and know that they were going through months of having to be in the hospital, some of them would never again be very strong or be able to do the active things that they had always done. I think my years at the hospital have meant a great deal to me because I learned so very much on how to take suffering. The men were so courageous and the women who were ill with their husbands far away and living, perhaps, in boarding houses were so brave that it has made me, perhaps, feel that a great deal of the fussing that people do over minor ailments is very unnecessary.

Q: Self-indulgence.

Mrs. N.: Self-indulgence. As Mary said to us yesterday, if you remember, it's through suffering that you grow, that you learn to accept your suffering, accept what you have to go through.

Q: In talking about her father?

Mrs. N.: Yes. In the evenings I spent frequently in San Francisco. They would call me in the morning and from the office of Mr. Cooley, who was running the war bonds, and say "Would you please write a talk for tonight to last three, four, five minutes, whatever it was, and come and broadcast it tonight?" So in the luncheon hour, I would sit there and write the talk that I was to give that night. They never bothered to read it beforehand because after the first two or three talks they discovered that I could do quite well on telling people why they needed to help the war bonds. So, for

Mrs. Nimitz #2 - 43

all those years I was broadcasting for them. In between I broadcast once or twice for OSS, and I broadcast to Burma, to the Philippines, to Australia, Christmas messages. I broadcast for the Women's Volunteer Service - WVS - I broadcast finally for, I think it was for, the Red Cross I did one broadcast. It seemed to me I got to where broadcasting did not worry me in the slightest. I could do it practically in my sleep.

Q: Without apprehension?

Mrs. N.: Yes. I remember once when we were broadcasting at the time when the United Nations was forming here in San Francisco, and I went over to do a broadcast. I was asked to do it by AWVS, a nationwide hook-up, where someone for Red Cross was going to speak from one place, someone for some other organization was speaking from another part of America, and just before the broadcast started a man called from New York and said to the man who was handling my broadcast, "Ask Mrs. Nimitz if she'll please help us out. Somebody's made a mistake, and we've got to have somebody talk for at least a minute more than was scheduled, and will she do it?" And I said to this man, "Well, if you'll toss the ball to me when I've finished talking about the AWVS and just say, 'Mrs. Nimitz, what else are you interested in in the way of organizations?' I will then take it from the Navy Relief." Which gave me a chance to get in on the Navy Relief. I was watching the clock and I finished at exactly the second I was supposed to at and inside of four minutes we got the most

Mrs. Nimitz #2 - 4

lovely call from New York thanking us for doing it. But I got to actually - I was - only once was I put on the air without, when I didn't expect to go on the air, and that was out in Sacramento, when I was out speaking for the war bonds and this very gorgeous young lady asked me if I would go on the air and I said, no, I don't like to go on unless I know what you're going to ask me, and she said, "Oh, I will just ask you very simple things. I won't really ask you anything that would be embarrassing." And I said, "Because I want to be careful." The first thing she asked me was, "How does your husband feel toward having to work with the Army?" And I was so angry. I answered her that my husband was in command of Army, Navy, Marine Corps, and Coast Guard, and he admired them equally. When I got off that thing, I just turned on her and gave her blazes. I said, "Of all the stupid remarks." Can you imagine?

Q: She had this in mind at the beginning.

Mrs. N.: I think the Admiral - when he would come in to see Admiral King, he would come home. Nobody knew he was coming. I usually knew it because he usually by letter would give me a hint that he would be in sometime. He would come to the house, and it was wonderful. The newspaper people respected absolutely the fact that he was not supposed to be here, that no one was to know it. And there was one woman who used to broadcast - who used to write for the Oakland Tribune - her name was Rose Glovinavich - and Rose never once broke a confidence. If she saw him with me or anything, she never mentioned a word

Mrs. Nimitz #2 - 45

until he was safely back in Honolulu that he had been here. But the little children on the street would be terribly excited when they would see the Admiral come in. They just couldn't get over it. They just hovered around.

Q: Was he in uniform then?

Mrs. N.: Yes, he was in uniform.

Q: How did he feel about all your broadcasting activity?

Mrs. N.: He didn't mind at all. He wasn't even thinking about me during the war. He was thinking about the war. Anything I wanted to do was all right. And I think I got a lot of money by telling these people, you feel that you are giving something. I got very angry in the Navy with the Navy's attitude that they had people trying to get the bluejackets to all buy bonds, you know.

Q: Yes.

Mrs. N.: Now, in a lot of cases, this was fine and saved the men money. But in other cases where they were men who had had more money before they came back into the Navy, you see, they were in businesses, so that their whole life had been set up on a different scale. Buying a bond or a half a bond a month sometimes put a terrible strain on their families. And in one or two cases where I saw that the wife was really in dire distress, I made them take it off. I just said to the men, "You just stop doing that. He can't afford to do that." There are limits.

Q: It's an interesting point of view. I mean where the standard of living had been prior to the war higher.

Mrs. N.: Yes, and then they had nothing. And then there was

always those who's standard of living was not higher at the beginning, but when you have a little girl living in one room with a new baby and having so terribly little to live on, going out and eating her meals at a lunch counter. And as I said once, (and I had them in tears before I finished,) I told 250 men in the Palace Hotel court, and I said to them, "What this means is, if she had that money, that 18 something that they were taking off for bonds, it meant the difference that perhaps when she went out to get her lunch and had a cup of coffee and a sandwich, she might have a little ice cream afterwards." I said, "I've seen these girls going without food that they desperately needed." And those men were out there taking all this fighting are being made to get bonds to help it through and I don't think it's right. I said, if they want to do it, if they are fixed in such a position that they can do it, this is fine, but there was terrible pressure put on them. Terrible pressure to buy bonds. I know because, I know that they came to me about it times. I was buying all the bonds for our family and I was living very simply and a gentlemen came and said he wanted to talk to me, and I said, "What about?" He said, "Well, I've just come back from the Pacific, and I've been trying to make your husband buy a bond a month, and he won't. He just said, "I'm not going to bother with the bonds." I said "No, he's not. I buy the bonds." And he said, "But I'd like him to buy the bonds because if he bought the bonds.." I said, My God, there's the whole Pacific to look out for. You want to make him do that? Are you crazy?" And he got furious with me and he said, "Well, I talked to another man whose wife was doing it for him and I made his wife agree to have him buy the bonds because it would look better that way. The way I did it with her was I sent her a big box of candy and she finally wrote and asked her husband to do it." I said, "Don't try anything like that on me because I will not ask my husband to buy the bonds. I'm buying the bonds for the family and I've bought over $10,000 worth, so that I wasn't cheating on anything." And he went out. He was a well-known person around Washington. And about three or four weeks later an enormous box of candy arrived and I never even unwrapped it. I took it just as it was up to the paraplegic ward and I said, "Look what I've got for you. Captain So-and-So in the Navy is sending you this lovely box of chocolates." And I said to the nurse, "I will write the thank-you letter." So I sat myself down and I wrote him and I said, "The box of chocolates which you so kindly sent to the paraplegic ward at the naval hospital was greeted with great cheers. They have asked me to thank you for it." Now, why did he want Admiral Nimitz? Just so he could say, I have everybody in the Pacific, for his own glorification. Because the bonds were being bought and Chester wasn't being bothered.

Q: Good for you.

Mrs. N.: This is the sort of thing that happens.

Q: And this takes courage, to take a stand like that.

Mrs. N.: No, I don't think it takes courage. I wouldn't have

Mrs. Nimitz #2 - 48

thought any other way, that was all. He just had to take it. Those four years while the Admiral was away and I had my daughter-in-law, who had been with me in Washington, was up in Vallejo. We are very close and she came west when I did. She would come down from Vallejo when Dad came to see him, and it was very nice to have her up there near me. She finally went back to Connecticut with my son when he came in from the last cruise that he did during the war, just before the end of the war, and they went back to the submarine base. There was a lot going on here during the war. It was very interesting and some San Francisco people were really wonderful in their attitudes, their attitude towards the people that came through, the sailors and the soldiers, they did a great deal for them, and the women worked so hard at the time when they were making what they called "Bundles for Britain." Those women would work day and night to get things to go to the British soldiers and to the families of them when they were having such a hard time. I was glad I was out here because when I went back to Washington at the end of the war, I sort of had the feeling that there were a great many people there that had never even realized the war was going on by their attitudes. They were still having the same social parties and all. We didn't have them out here. People were busy. And by the time night came you weren't interested in anything except getting to bed. Chester would come in every so often. He would get in and we'd have a chance to talk during the evening and then the next morning he'd go over to meet

Mrs. Nimitz #2 - 49

with King and talk all day, and then he'd come back at night and probably take off that night and go back to Honolulu. He came in once, you know, and was dumped into the Bay, and I was down there watching him. He was coming into Alameda and the plane...

Q: A flying boat?

Mrs. N.: Yes. The plane turned over. I think one man was killed. Admiral McCormick had his back broken. I remember when my husband came ashore he was still clutching his brief case. He'd come out through the bow of the plane, and he was soaking wet and Admiral Greenslade was there with his aide and so we helped Chester into my car and I was living at that time at the Hotel Durant in Berkeley. It was in the very first part of my stay out here, and I was staying at the Hotel Durant, and we rushed Chester in and I said, "Let's take the elevator from the basement up because I don't want to take my husband looking like a drowned rat, soaking, dripping wet, up to the main floor." So we took the elevator and we didn't let it stop. The boy went all the way to where my room was. We took the Admiral right into a hot bath and while he was sitting in the hot bath, the Admiral's aide, Admiral Greenslade's aide, went out and bought him some underwear - dry underwear. We finally got his clothes dried out because we were not allowed to stay in Berkeley when we - when the Admiral came the first few times we took him to a hotel in San Francisco which had been taken over by the service, and we were whisked up to the eighth floor where he was kept

Mrs. Nimitz #2 - 50

absolutely - no one could get onto the floor. They had Marines at all the exits and entrances. So as soon as we could get him dry enough and get his clothes dried off to get over - then the doctor came to check him over and insisted on him turning in for the rest of the day for fear he would...

Q: Was he shaken up by this?

Mrs. No.: No. I've never seen anybody come through all sorts of things calmly as he did.

Q: You were a fine pair, weren't you?

Mrs. N.: He was absolutely calm about this whole thing. He said - er, he was still clutching his bag and I was awfully glad to get him over there and get him quiet for a little while. He stayed in bed for that afternoon, and the next day he said, "I'm not going to stay in bed any more," and he went for his meeting with the Admiral. I think - I don't know whether - yes, Admiral King must have been here that day. Then in the afternoon he put on civilian clothes and he said, let's go down, and let's walk on the streets and have some window shopping and so forth. So we took a nice walk and we got to the foot of the hill of California Street and decided to take the cable car up to the top and go and call on Admiral and Mrs McColough. He was a delightful man who had just retired in the Navy and he and his wife were great friends of ours. Anyway, we took the cable car up to the top and just as we got to the stop where we were going to get off,

Mrs. Nimitz #2 - 51

the people about to get on the cable car were Commander McCondry, who had been with Chester at the University of California and was a great friends of mine, a most charming bachelor, and his mother. He saw Chester and he was terribly excited. He didn't say who he was, but he whispered to his mother, "He's Admiral Nimitz," and his mother was so excited. We were just getting off and we were standing there and finally McCondry and his mother got on the car. The cable man was getting frantic, you see, because this conversation was going on and the cable car was being held up. McCondry and his mother got on and McCondry said he nearly died laughing after it got started. He said in a loud voice, not to McCondry but to the whole car, "And who does that man think he is holding up the car like this?" McCondry said "I was dying to say, well you'd be surprised if you knew who it was.'

Q: And so you did these little things just to have a bit of normal life?

Mrs. N.: Yes, we'd go round and see our friends whenever we'd get a chance.

Q: It was therapeutic for him.

Mrs. N.: Yes, very much so because he knew that I had made tremendous numbers of friends here in San Francisco. Friends that since then have become oh so close to us. Wonderful friends. Anyway, I could see his intention was that in the long run we would be coming back here to live.. He never wanted to go back to Texas. He wanted to come back here.

Because he left Texas, what few Texans realize is that he left Texas when he was 15, and his whole life has been a life around the ocean. I think if he hadn't had a long view he would have been a most unhappy man. I remember when we were looking for a house, he said to me, "I have just one stipulation. It is to have three bathrooms and a long view. I don't want to share a bathroom with my grandchildren always." So we got a house with three bathrooms and a long view.

Interview #3 with Mrs. Chester W. Nimitz

By John T. Mason, Jr.

Date: 6 June 1969

Place: Her apartment in San Francisco

Q: Mrs. Nimitz, you want, I think, to read some excerpts from a diary which sounds most fascinating.

Mrs. N.: This is a description of the day on which the Admiral relinquished the Chief of Naval Operations command and we started for the West Coast. The Admiral had always said, "When it comes time for me to give up my job here, we get out on that day. We are not going to stay around and breathe down the next man's neck." So we left on the 15th of December 1947, following the change of command, and this is the description that we both wrote in a diary which we were then starting to keep of our time from then on. We called it "Life Begins at 117," because at that time that was our combination of ages.

Q: And, of course, he adhered strictly to the regulations during the war time and didn't keep a diary.

Mrs. N.: Yes. He couldn't keep a diary. My entry was the first one and it says:

Scandia Cottage, 7 miles north of Raleigh on Highway 1 - U.S. Highway 1.

This has been a momentous day. The great event has taken place and tonight, despite rain and cold air, we are happy. For the first time in many years, Chester has little responsibility.

Nancy, Freckles, Chester, and I are headed south, then west to California, and our hearts are young and gay. Nancy at the moment is not too gay as she has a tummy ache. We arrived here at 4.50 p.m. in a downpour with mud under foot. Our cabins are warm and comfortable so we have no complaints. We arose and breakfasted as usual at 7. During breakfast we called Romerez and the rest of the staff into the dining room. Chester made a nice little speech of appreciation and good wishes to them, and we handed them their Christmas money.

Chester left for the office at the usual time. Chase and Ogle came early to say goodbye. They have been very faithful and we appreciated all they have done. As I left, the boys were busy washing finger marks off doors and putting the finishing touches on cleaning up. Tonight the Denfelds are living there...

Q: This was in Observatory House?

Mrs. N.: Yes, this was in Observatory House.

...May they have real happiness in the CNO house. Mrs. Denfeld loves flowers which makes me very ahppy. At 2222 Q Street I gathered Nancy and her bag. She took over the wheel to drive to the Navy Department. The turnover and the getaway I want Chester to write. He was one of the principal actors. It is wonderful to be together bound for California and home. As I said to several this morning, my clothes did not have the "new look" but I do.

This part is written by the Admiral:

The attached memos give the turnover procedure as planned, but as usual something occurred to upset the plan. Instead of having the movies and so forth before the ceremony, that chore came at 10.10, after Denfeld had relieved me. This change was necessitated by reason of a conference at 10.40 by the Secretary and Mr. Webb, director of the Budget, and Mr. Sullivan needed a briefing from his own subordinates on the conference agenda, which was the shipbuilding program for the fiscal year of 1948.

Despite changed plans, we got off at 10.30, exactly as we had previously planned. Many out of town officers came for the turnover, including Spruance, Blandy, and so forth. I was particularly pleased to have present in the SecNav's office my family, Catherine and Nancy, and Mr. and Mrs. Kurt C. Schiffler, Captain Walter Carreck [Carey], USNR, who limped in on a cane from Bethesda Naval Hospital, Father Sheehy, Chaplain Corps, and many others. The Secretary's office was filled to overflowing and many people were in the hall. Secretary Sullivan made a brief but very laudatory address, after which I addressed the group. The copy of the address is attached. (He didn't attach it.) Then I read my orders. The Denfelds, my successor at CNO, read his orders and made a brief address, following which the Secretary gave him his commission. Then the SecNav with commendable respect for the schedule, took us rapidly through another large office, where the movies, sound included, were awaited - were waiting - along with numerous stillphotographers. Ten minutes were consumed in taking and "just one more," after which we moved on outwards towards the main entrance, Constitution Avenue....

Q: How did he respond to the "just one mores?"

Mrs. N.: He'd learnt patience...

We moved out toward the main entrance of Constitution Avenue through throngs of officers, civilians, service men of all branches, to our car. The Navy band and the Marine guard gave the presented honors and so we embarked in our car with Nancy at the wheel. It was a moving demonstration of genuine good will from a great many friends and well-wishers we have in Washington. Among those present was Senator Saltonstall, representatives Plumley, Sheppard, and some others whose names I could not remember. I feel as if a great burden had been lifted from my shoulders, and that Catherine and I are just beginning to live with a wonderful family of children and grandchildren, and with the world before us. How can we fail to have a full and happy life before us. I could write reams more, but I am sure my readers can understand my feelings of genuine relief at having passed the burden to younger shoulders.

I thought that was very nice.

Q: That note of sincerity certainly comes through there. He was truly glad to...

Mrs. N.: He was very glad. [TIRED]

Q: It seemed like a bit of an anticlimax, didn't it, to be CNO after being CincPac?

Mrs. N.: No, I don't think it was an anticlimax. I think that he had an entirely different type of problem in trying to squeeze the Navy down a little and to get things into proportion again. And I think Truman was very helpful to him. Truman backed him very well indeed. He had a great deal of affection for President Truman and he always said that eventually history would show him to be one of our great presidents. Truman had great guts.

Q: Yes, he did. Not so terribly polished...

Mrs. N.: Not polished, but they were a delightful pair. We were very fond of both of them. They came up to the house to pitch horse shoes one afternoon, and it was such fun because, of course, the secret service had come up the day before and they came in to me and said, "Oh, this is the most wonderful thing, we don't have to do a thing. For a few hours tomorrow afternoon, we can relax. You have Marines at all the gates and nobody's going to get in." Well, the Trumans arrived and he went up and put on one of Chester's old khaki pants and we all four went down to pitch horse shoes. I must admit that he was not a good horse-shoe pitcher.

Q: He wasn't? He was out of practice.

Mrs. N.: No. Mrs. Truman was much better and so they won. Mrs. Truman and Chester played the President and myself. But we had great fun doing it and then we started wandering up the side lawn toward the house where we had an apple tree that had magnificent apples on it. Well, we stopped under there and they ate apples off the tree, and then they thought they were such wonderful-flavored apples that we got the mess boys and told them to get a great big sack and fill it with the apples. Then we walked all over the yard, and it was so nice because there was nobody following. They were just free. We went up to see this magnificent oak tree which was on the grounds of the Observatory, and Chester showed it to them because he was very fond of trees and was very conscious of the beauty of this great oak. And then we went in and had high balls and I remember that when it got time for the Trumans to leave, the boys brought the bag of apples out and Mrs. Truman leaned over and said to the driver, "Now, I want it understood this bag of apples is not to go into the kitchen. It's to go up to our bedroom. We're going to eat these apples." We saw a great deal of the Trumans while we were there and had so many pleasant recollections. She used to love to get my stories, so they quite frequently were at the symphony or places like that. They put us next to the Trumans because that relieved them of worrying about the next box - who was in the next box.

Q: We had security there.

Mrs. N.: Yes.

Q: You say she loved to hear your stories?

Mrs. N.: Oh, yes. I remember one night when the San Francisco Symphony was going to play so Chester and I took a box and they immediately said, do you mind if we put the Trumans in the box next to you because that will make it easier for everybody. I said, no, I'd love it, and at the beginning of the evening

Mrs. Nimitz - 59

when the Trumans came in, Mrs. Truman leaned over and said, "Please sit close to my box. I want to hear some more stories."

Q: What kind of stories did you tell her?

Mrs. N.: Well, now, that is between Mrs. Truman and myself.

Q: Were they the kind the Admiral told?

Mrs. N.: Yes, certainly, and Mrs. Truman loved them. We spent a delightful day up in the Sonoma Valley when we came north to hunt for a house as the guests of Hap Arnold and his wife, and they had a lovely ranch up there and we went...

Q: This was at the end of the trip that began in Washington?

Mrs. N.: Yes. Well, it was about a month or two afterwards, when we came up to San Francisco and we were staying at the Fairmont. We went up to see the Arnolds. The Arnolds sent their car for us, and we went up there, and one man offered us the land free, five acres free, and he would build our house at cost if we would only come up to that side. That was the side of the valley where the Cooks were living...

Q.: A beautiful part.

Mrs. N.: Yes, but we didn't like it because it was too hilly. We wanted more level land. Then we went over to another builder who was terribly interested in our taking 25 acres in the old Spreckles - big Spreckles ranch, and that was just the most enchanting area and we very nearly took that....

Q: Would that have given the Admiral the long view?

Mrs. N.: But not the long view of the sea, and I think he would have been unhappy not seeing it because he was so happy being able to look out of the window of our place in Berkeley and see the sea.

Q: I thought that was what you meant by the long view, the sea.

Mrs. N.: Yes. It was, and you see he wouldn't have had it - no, the view up there would have been beautiful, but there would have been a stop point to it.

Q: Landlocked?

Mrs. N.: Landlocked, and that was why we finally decided on the house in Berkeley. And speaking of settling in the house at Berkeley, I must say there was a very funny side to that. The Admiral was suddenly realizing that he wasn't - didn't have anything that had to be done each day, and it was sort of getting him down, and we were staying at the Hotel Claremont in Berkeley, and I was looking for houses. We both had been looking for houses, down on the peninsula which was where I wanted to live, and several other places. So finally, one day, the agent called up and said that there was a house to rent for the summer because Chester had gotten to the point where he felt he had to get out of the hotel, As was quite normal. PEOPLE WHO HAD LOST SONS OUT IN THE Pacific and who were at the hotel would come up while we were breakfasting or something and say, "Admiral, I just want to speak to you. My son was killed out in the Pacific," and so forth, and this was getting him down a little bit because it's hard to have your meals interrupted with people telling you their sorrows when you are trying to relax in peace. So, I finally decided we'd try to rent a house for the summer if we couldn't do anything else, but I didn't want to. I wanted to buy a house, because if we rented it we had to stay out the length of time, and this one house the lady said she was sure I would like it. She took me to see it. Chester was going back to his office that morning. And I got out, in the first place there was about 50 to 75 steps going up to the house, which finished it as far as I was concerned. Secondly, when I got in the house and looked at it, it was filled with blown-glass animals with all sorts of knick-knacks on every place you could look. It was quite obvious by looking at that house that there never was a child in it and there never was a dog in there. Then the price they asked at that time for the house I knew was a price put up for the benefit of a fleet admiral and was about twice as high as they could possibly have gotten at that time from anybody else. So I looked around and I said, "Well, of course, I have to tell you that we have a dog," and the man sort of shivered and said, "A dog?" I said, yes. So he said, "I don't know but perhaps a Fleet Admiral's dog is better behaved than most dogs." I saw that wasn't going to work and I thought rapidly, what can I say now, and I got a bright idea. I said, "I have six grandchildren and they're all coming to spend the summer with us." So he said he was very sorry but he couldn't rent the house to us, which was what I wanted, and we quickly left, and the lady who had taken me up there to look at it was very distressed over this. She had thought that this was a sure thing. So after we got away from there she said in sort of a hopeless way, "You wouldn't care to look at a house to buy, would you?" I said what was the price, then I said, "Oh, we can't possibly afford that house. What's the use of looking at it?" She said, "Well, would you just look at it?" And I said, yes, feeling that I'd really done her in, I'd look at it. So I was taken to look at this house. I looked at the outside of it and it was a charming, Spanish-type house, on top of a hill, and the view from it was magnificent. It looked entirely over San Francisco Bay. It couldn't have been more beautiful. I went all through the place. The Admiral had always said that one thing he had to have was a long view and three bath rooms. The three bath romms was because he said he didn't like the idea of sharing bath rooms with his grandchildren. So, this house had a long view and three bath rooms, and it was in absolutely perfect condition because the man who owned it also owned a paint factory, and the combination was wonderful. I asked them how much it was and said I would talk to my husband, and when I got back I called him, he was in his office in San Francisco, and said, "I think I've got your house for you. I think you'd really better come home and take a look at it quick, because I think this is just exactly what you're talking about." So I took him out there and I could see that he was just thrilled with it. So he said, "But we can't afford that price." And I said, no, and the woman said, "They're awfully anxious to get out of that house. Why don't you just make them an offer?" So we made them an offer, over $10,000 less than what they were asking for, and by night, she had called Chicago, got in touch with her husband, and we were told we could have the house. They came back with a different offer, which we decided to accept. That was how we bought our house on Santa Barbara Road in Berkeley. We called it Long View, and the Admiral was so crazy to get into this house that he positively pushed those people out. In fact, they were going out the front door and he was taking me in the back door. He was just frantic to get in there and get his home started.

Q: His home.

Mrs. N.: Just home, and he had a beautiful sun dial which had been designed for him by a former blue jacket and who had been famous for making perfect sun dials. So he had much to do and much to get started with. The first thing he discovered was that the people who were living in it had no bookcases. I only saw one book during my entire cruise through the house, so we knew that that was the first order of business, to have tremendous bookshelves installed in all the rooms. In the living room, one whole end was devoted to books. In my study the whole side of the place was put over to books, and for the others we bought bookcases for each room, so that each room had many books in it. I think that the complete satisfaction that the Admiral had when he got into that house was delightful.

Q: And the garden was magnificent, wasn't it?

Mrs. N.: The garden was lovely, and we were very fortunate. Our first Japanese gardener was a charming young man and he worked for us very well and while we were away the first time he took care of it. Then he married and went to live in another town, and then we got the really wonderful character of Tad Hikayago [Hikiago], who is one of the really wonderful Americans. He was in that, I think it was the Four-Forty, which was made up of Nisei that were in Europe in the war, and he had such a magnificent record all through the war. We loved Tad dearly, both Chester and I. He would be working away on the lawn and I'd say, "Tad, it's coffee time," and he would come in and sit and talk to Chester and myself. He was the straightest thinking American that you can imagine, and the way he brought his children up, they were straight-thinking Americans. We dearly loved that man and he dearly loved the house. As far as I know, he's still taking care of it, but very unhappy about the situation because the people who bought it after we left were not very interested in gardens and they rented the house for two years to some Chilean people, who were not interested in gardens at all, not interested in raising a finger to do anything, and the people that bought the house would only have Tad one morning a week, which was not nearly enough, and they would not water the place in between, so that Tad was very unhappy over it.

Q: Did the Admiral like flowers? Did he do anything himself?

Mrs. N.: Oh, the Admiral was a mad gardener. He gardened entirely and he built compost heaps, and the soil that he finally got for that place was the most beautiful soil I've ever seen. You could crumble it so beautifully. And he took such pride in things that he planted. He had a little bit of a tendency like the German gardener I had had during the war, if he liked what I wanted to plant the things grew magnificently, but if I planted something he didn't like, it was surprising how rapidly it could go. And I think that was a little the Admiral's attitude. If he liked what I planted, it grew; if he didn't...

Q: He put a curse on it, uh?

Mrs. N.: ...it faded, didn't do so well.

Q: Now, tell me about that house, I mean when you were looking for houses, the house you described with the concrete floors.

Mrs. N.: Well, there was some man wrote to us, I wish I could find it, Can you shut it off a minute and let me find it? During this period where we had been house-hunting, at 10:30 ...

Q: Is this your description or the Admiral's?

Mrs. N.: This is my description. At 10:30 one evening, a special delivery came to us telling of a most unique and awful house. The owner and builder proudly announced it was made entirely of ships' hatch covers welded together, with concrete floors, even the walls and partitions were hatch covers. It gave me a good laugh.

Q: What did it give the Admiral?

Mrs. N.: Oh, yes, the Admiral was a little shocked at the idea.

Q: Was this a former serviceman?

Mrs. N.: I don't know. It doesn't say here and I don't remember. I just remember his description of it. I believe it was - an ex-sailor or chief petty officer.

Q: He really thought this was pleasing.

Mrs. N.: Yes, he thought that we might enjoy having it. The Admiral was made an honorary member of the Bohemian Club in San Francisco, one of the very few who - I think a King of Sweden and President Roosevelt and the Admiral, no I don't think there were any, I don't know who else. But he described his Bohemian big party that they gave for him...

Q: That's that lovely club up near the Clift Hotel?

Mrs. N.: Yes. He enjoyed the club but he did not go up to the encampment but once, and in that time when he was up at that encampment he was in the area where ex-President Hoover was, and Paul Smith of The Chronicle and a great many other people. But it was too close to the time of the war and Chester found there was no rest up there for him. He couldn't go down to the river for a swim that people on all sides would ask him to come in to their camp...

Q: A summer encampment there with several hundred people, aren't there?

Mrs. N.: Yes, and I think one of the reasons that he did not go back again was because at that time he was coming down with the 'flu. He didn't recognize it at the time, but after a few days he came home and went to bed, and he had a very bad case of 'flu.

Q: So the grove had an unpleasant association.

Mrs. Nimitz - 67

Mrs. N.: No, the grove didn't have an unpleasant association. It had a very pleasant association with him, inasmuch as he met many, many people that he had known in Washington and that he had known through the war, and that he had known out here. And he enjoyed being with them, but he said that the hospitality was such that he said,"I just - I just can't take so much hospitality when I'm trying to have a rest and vacation." But he really loved the Bohemian Club in town and he used to love to take people to lunch there.

Q: It looks like a beautiful place. Do you have the description of it that he wrote?

Mrs. N.: Let me see, now, I ought to. I can't locate it. That's what I was doing when you came in, trying to find it. Oh, here it is: "At 6 p.m. - this was on January 15th, 1948 - I picked up Bruce Canaga, (Bruce Canaga was Captain Canaga in the Navy and Chester's most - the man in his class that he was most fond of.) and went to San Francisco to the Bohemian Club where a dinner was being given by the Club President, President Fred W. Pabst, and the sire (?) Armor Rock (Almar Rock, I guess it is) in my honor. Some 400 members were present, including many old friends and shipmates from the war. Excellent dinner. Excellent entertainment which included Rudi Seger with his violin and Yuda Waldrop with the piano, who played three numbers, the last, California Lullaby, Rudi's own composition. The last refrain was accompanied by a man's voice somewhere in the darkened room, and the effect was marvelous. (It's a beautiful piece, California Lullaby.) Then came my turn. A brief speech at the table, which included some new stories which the members seemed to relish, and then I was called to the dining room stage and given a test to see where I fitted in and what I could do as an actor. While I had on an Indian headdress and blanket, I was both on receiving and giving end of card tricks. My mentors finally decided I was fit only to carry a spear, so with spear and toga I lead the band out of the dining room and down to the cartoon room, which is also the bar room, where I met many new people and where I was presented with a large cartoon of myself which had been signed along the margin by many Bohemians. Bruce Canaga and I got away about 11 p.m. and returned to our homes in Berkeley. Will be glad when these parties end so we can pursue our house-hunting more seriously. Found mother still awake and had probably spent part of the evening letter-writing."

He enjoyed these parties terrifically, but he had - at that time the one thing he wanted in the world was to get a house, and get into a place where we were on our own, where we were not in a hotal where people could reach us, and for several years after we went to Berkeley our house telephone number was unlisted.

Q: He refers there to some new stories. Where did he get these stories? Did he compose them himself?

Mrs. N.: I don't know, but he always had the most fabulous stock of stories, and they were delightful stories. There was one that he used to tell about the - he always loved this story and I was at a dentist's office not too long ago and somebody said, "You remember the story that your husband used to tell about the race track," and I thought back and I believe that I heard him tell that story and I've always loved it. It was the story of the little, the Minister's wife, who was leading a very dull life and her husband was away at the time, and they had so little money and the next-door neighbors were going to the race track and they came over to this little lady and said, "Won't you go down to the race track with us this afternoon. You don't have to bet or anything like that, but we think that you don't get out half enough. We'll take you down and just sit you in the stand and you can watch these beautiful horses run. And sit in the sun and it will be very good for you." She was very doubtful but she hadn't been out and she was lonely, so she said yes, she would, she didn't know whether her husband would approve of it, but she would go. So they went down to the track and these friends of hers would leave her and rush up and make a bet and come back. And she got rather caught up in this after a while, She had the program and she was looking at the different races and finally she saw coming up a race with one of the horses in the race named Leviticus. Now this was a Bible name and she felt that it was a very important name and she began to get itchy. So after the other couple had rushed off to put their bets in, she looked in her bag and she did have two dollars, so she slipped up when no one was looking, and after they had left the window, and she said to the man, "Two dollars on Leviticus," and they gave her a ticket. Well, Leviticus was a 100 to 1 shot, he was expected to come in last in the race, and she didn't tell anyone she had the ticket, and she went down and she sat and watched. And of course, miracles do happen, and Leviticus must have been inspired by the thought that the woman was there and betting on him, for he ran so well that he won the race, and then she realized that she was to go up. She wasn't quite sure how much money she was going to get, but she knew she had won, and she'd seen the others coming back with two dollars and a half or three dollars and a half. So she went up and collected, to her absolute astonishment and rather to her agony of mind, $200, and she put it in her bag and she was very concerned about the thing. Her friends were just delighted. They thought this poor soul never has anything, now she's got a little bit of money to spend. She went home and the next night when her husband came back from the mission trip that he'd been on, she knew she had to tell him, so she blurted out that she had gone to the races and that she had - well she'd just fallen, she couldn't resist betting on this horse. The minister was human. He was deadly sick of hamburger every night, and he said, "Well, darling, all right, we'll keep the money. We can undoubtedly do good with some of it. But," he said, "you know those race track people they're low class, they're uneducated. You shouldn't have anything to do with them." And she said, "Oh, darling, you're absolutely wrong. They're not badly educated. The people

I talked to were very educated." He said, "What do you mean, very educated?" "Well," she said, "When I put my ticket in the window to get my money, the man looked at it and he turned to the man behind him and he said, 'Jesus, Marcus, Leviticus wrecked us.'" This was one of the Admiral's choicest.

Q: I've heard from various people that he was very fond of and very able at telling stories.

Mrs. N.: He was very able at telling stories and once in a while he would start telling a story and I'd say no, and he'd look at me with a wicked expression on his face, and I'd say no. Then he would stop. But it was when he didn't know the people present and I did, and I knew that one person was going to be very offended by the story.

Q: When he made a public speech, did he introduce it with a story?

Mrs. N.: He would very frequently tell a story and get everybody with him because his stories were just fabulous. There's one I'll tell you when we're not on tape.

Q: I tried to get Freeman to tell me some of them on tape, but he wouldn't.

Mrs. N.: The period when we came back here to live, back to this area, had so much fun with it because as Regent of the University we saw so much of the people at the University, and we went about, we had to go to Riverside campus for University meets, and I loved dearly to swim, so that I would swim in the pool in the old Mission Inn down there. It was is a very famous inn. I believe, I think it has had to be closed now. It was so terribly old and the upkeep was terrifically high. I'm not perfectly certain it's closed but it seems to me I've been told it was. We would go there and to Los Angeles, to Santa Barbara when Santa Barbara was just being thought of, and go over the area which was the old Marine base in that area. We knew the Berkeley campus and he would go up to the Davis campus. I didn't even go up there with him because it was just a daytime trip. But we met such intelligent, delightful people, and in so many walks of life. We knew the Lawrences, ~~Don~~ John and Edward, particularly Edward Lawrence, and we were very fond of him because when Chester was the head of the Atomic Energy Committee at the University - of the committee that the Regents were on - we went up from Los Angeles to Los Alamos on a train and among those present on the train was Edward Lawrence and we had great fun with him all the way up. Then they lived close to us in Berkeley, so we saw them many times. He was a stupendous person and just the most wonderful person to know. There were so many of those people at the University. Bob Sproul and Ida, his wife. They were both delightful people to know and, of course, they are still my friends. Pauley was a Regent then. I think Pauley has just retired from the Regency. Mrs. Hearst came on toward the end of Chester's stay there. And the woman from Los Angeles whose husband used to be the head of the <u>Los Angeles Times</u>. She took it over. Mrs. Chandler. She is a very wonderful woman and has done so much for the Los Angeles area with the music center and all that. Now her son is running the <u>Los Angeles Times</u> and I must admit I think it's probably the best paper on the West Coast by all odds. Chester enjoyed all the people, the Nobel prize winners and the people that had a great many interests in life. They're rather delightful people to be with because accomplishments...

Q: They're alive...

Mrs. N.: Yes, and at that time the Griller Quartet was here from England, and as my son was at the - my son came out to be executive officer of the ROTC, he played the violin and his mother-in-law was living with them at that time and she was a professional. She played both violin and viola.

Q: Joan's mother?

Mrs. N.: Yes, Joan's mother. So we had a wonderful time because my son was so impressed the first time he heard the Griller Quartet that he wrote them a note, and they were so pleased with this note that they invited him to come up to their rehearsals at the University, because they were going to be the quartet in residence at the University as well as play all over the country. Then the Grillers, after we had bought our house, bought a house just about a block from us and we had such fun with that quartet and with the Griller family and the Nimitz family. And a very charming relationship grew up between the Admiral and the little Griller girl who was about 12. She loved to come over to the house with us, and when her family would be going out of an evening and had to leave Catherine, Catherine said to the Admiral that they left her with awfully dull people. So Chester got the hint immediately and said to the Grillers, "When you go out leave Catherine with us," which was just wonderful. Catherine would come from school and stay with us, and the Admiral would spoil her to death. He would take her wherever she wanted to go and she could make cake if she wanted to, we did all sorts of things, and the next day instead of walking to school, he took her to school. He had a marvelous time and during that period something happened when one day and he fixed a zipper for her in a dress because he had a little gadget that could fix zippers, which he had done for me. One afternoon when we were entertaining some people - I think it was some distinguished people from the University or from the Navy, we could see Catherine Griller coming in the drive walk holding something in her hand. She rushed up to the door and she said, "Admiral, I've got to have this zipper in my red pants fixed and I can't go until I can have it fixed." So Chester went and got his arrangement and fixed the zipper for Catherine. And that friendship has lasted through many years. The Grillers are now in London. The quartet has been given up. But we had a very delightful time because they would come and practise in our house. They would bring people like Primorse who played the viola so magnificently, and they would come down and do their practising for concerts in our house because our living room was big. So we met these people. We were very close to Pierre Monteux and his wife and to...

Q: Where did you get in touch with them?

Mrs. N.: Well, during the war when I was here, the only social life I had, I'd let myself go to the symphony. I would buy two season tickets and then when I couldn't use them I'd give them to sailors at the hospital to use. And through that I got to know, oh, most of the people interested in the musical life of the city. Leonore Almsby who's done - who was really the backbone of the symphony at the start and she was also a beautiful musician. And when the big visiting artist came I would go back to meet them and I got to be very much interested and a part of the symphony. Then when Chester and I came back, we also always had two symphony tickets. And all of these people - we went to the parties with all of them and the Admiral dearly loved the symphony, but he loathed most modern music, and it got to be a joke because when the orchestra would come in and we were sitting about three rows back, because the Admiral wanted to be right down where he could watch them...

Q: I don't blame him. I like that, too.

Mrs. N.: ...and we'd be sitting there, and there'd be a modern piece of music of music coming up and you'd see all the symphony players looking over at the Admiral, then they'd look at me and begin to laugh, because they'd know that he was going to be thoroughly disgusted. And one delightful incident happened one afternoon. We went in and sat down in our seats and Chester was looking at his program and he turned to me and he said, "This is going to be just beautiful." And he pointed to the first symphony that was to be played. He wasn't enough familiar with these composers to note the difference in the first name of it. And the first symphony that was to be played was William Schuman's symphony, a most modern piece, and I noted it immediately and I thought, oh, boy, this is going to be wonderful. Well, the symphony started and a puzzled look came on the Admiral's face, very puzzled. He listened a little longer and he looked accusingly at the musicians, then he took out his program and looked at it again and didn't say a word. When it was over he looked at me and said just one word, "William." Well, we were dining that night with the conductor and several members of the symphony orchestra, and I told this story, and I thought they would die laughing. And after that they'd say to each other when something would be coming up, "William." But the Admiral really had such love of music and he loved...

Q: Who were his first favorites?

Mrs. N.: His favorite composer was Brahms symphony, the fourth Brahms symphony and the first and second he loved dearly. He loved a lot of other pieces, but the Brahms symphony...During the war the only present - we never sent him any presents, but we sent him fine records because this was a great relief to him before dinner at night. The aide knew enough to get up and start the victrola with some symphony records. And then the people in San Francisco got to sending him beautiful records. We had the most beautiful collection of records autographed by Monteux and by people like that, which we eventually - they were 78 records - and we eventually gave them to Arnold Griller, the son of the violinist, because he is now - Mr. Griller Senior, is now the head of the violin section of the Royal Academy. Our musical life here in San Francisco was really delightful. We went to symphonies all the time. We went to a great many operas, which I think Chester slept through most of them, but he enjoyed the dinners before and he enjoyed the people he went with. And he enjoyed some of the operas very much.

Q: He really was, at times, almost a social butterfly, wasn't he?

Mrs. N.: Oh, while we were here in San Francisco, yes. We had a very lovely social life - wonderful social life - with delightful people - with the Walter Haases, with Mrs. Haas's mother, Mrs. Sigmund Stern, who died a few years ago, with the Sidney Ehrmans, with all the people in the musical world, especially Dr. John Upton and Mrs. Upton, and Mrs. Upton's sister, Mrs. Margaret St. Alban, we were very fond of. We saw a great deal and we used to have parties all around at these different places, and I must tell you an amusing story. On Chester's birthday Mrs. Stern was giving a beautiful dinner for him and I assure you her dinners were something out of this world, with enormous ice pieces in the center with the American eagle, absolutely gorgeous decorations, and always the Gradys were there. Henry Grady was amabassador to India, to Iran, and Greece. Mrs. Grady was a Spanish girl, whose family was from the first Spanish settlers in California. Very beautiful, very vivacious, very gay, and very determined

Mrs. Nimitz - 77A

to handle things. But a just delightful person. At this particular dinner, during the dinner it happened that Harry Grady and I were usually put as partners, and he turned to me at the beginning of dinner and said, "You know, the doctors told me this afternoon I had to be in the hospital - I had to go right to the hospital from the doctors' office and I said, no, I'm going to make the speech at Chester's dinner tonight and I'm not going to the hospital. I'm going back there and make that speech, and, he said, you have to be in there tonight because you've got a very serious heart condition." So I knew the Gradys didn't have an automobile, and as we always picked them up, I got my husband's attention and said to him that Henry was having to go to the hospital right after dinner and could he get word to Cozard to come and drive him. So Cozard came to drive Henry Grady to the hospital, and Walter Haas went with them to see Henry safely installed in the hospital. But they told me afterwards that Henry Grady said that when they got to the hospital, Cozard said goodbye to him and as he got out, he said, "Mr. Grady, if you don't like the hospital, Sally Stanford's is just two doors up the street." Sally Stanford's being the leading madame in San Francisco.

Q: Quite a different therapy.

Mrs. N.: Different therapy, but he was so funny. These were the people that we were with constantly, that we did things with, that we went around with, and that we enjoyed immensely, and the last birthday party that the Admiral had on the island

Mrs. Nimitz - 78

was the year - he died in '66 - was in '65.

Q: That was his 80th birthday?

Mrs. N.: Yes, and he hadn't been out of the hospital very long, but we asked all of these people, and I think there was a young - not young Russian, but a Russian that was fitted in with our group called Pom de Raffine [Pume Delagene crossed out] who came to the party with us...

Q: You'll have to spell that.

Mrs. N.: Yes, but anyway this was a very gay party and the Haases brought sailors' caps for everybody, white sailors' caps, and Mr. Haas gave a very pleasant talk of the Admiral - [in memory of the Admiral crossed out] because of his birthday. It was a very gay party, and that was the last birthday party because from the time we came here until then, Chester's birthday and Mrs. Stern's, as long as she lived, we always celebrated, the whole group, together. And such beautiful parties as we had at Mrs. Stern's beautiful home.

Q: I have a clipping still at home of the Admiral on his 80th birthday. It appeared in The New York Times. He was in a dark-colored shirt. A very good portrait of him.

Mrs. N.: Yes. One of our mess boys who had a marvelous sense of humor, Estobal, said to me the next day, "You know, I was just (because the Admiral wore his uniform, the others were in evening dress) - when they gave the Admiral a sailor cap to put on his head," he said, "I was just itching to call the patrol and say there's someone out of uniform at the Admiral's house. You'd better come up and get him."

Well, this part of our life out here was tremendously delightful. Of course, we had a break of two years when we went back to the United Nations.

Q: Tell me first, since you made mention before of your great love of swimming, and he obviously was a great swimmer himself. Tell me something about that.

Mrs. N.: Well, as a matter of fact, in the later years he did very little swimming because of his ears...

(Interruption)

Q: The Admiral did not swim very much?

Mrs. N.: Yes. Because of danger to his ears. You see, when he was a young submarine officer, he had an abcess in his ear when he was at sea, and the pain got so bad that finally he washed out one of the syringes that they used on the engines and washed out his ear with it. His hearing was never very good, that was always a problem, so he didn't like to swim so much. So I was the great swimmer while we were on the island - towards the end and on my 73rd birthday down in the pool on the island I swam a mile, to the absolute edification of a few sailors that were there, and one of them in charge of the pool. This was an Olympic-sized pool. And there was one young sailor who had to qualify to go on a ship. He had to swim the length of the pool, and he just struggled to reach the end of the pool, when I dove in and started swimming and he would watch me. I'd go up to the end of the pool and swim back again and after about the fifth time, he was shaking his head, but when it came to the 32nd time he was just...stunned. So that

Mrs. Nimitz - 80

I did more swimming than the Admiral towards the end, because I enjoyed it tremendously.

Q: Well, my reference was because of the number of times I had heard about him swimming during the war when he and Admiral Spruance would go on their afternoon exercises and the exercises included walking three miles down the beach and then swimming one mile back.

Mrs. N.: Yes, well I think that he probably did during the war, but after the war he didn't do so much swimming. We'd go down to the Cape and he'd go in and take a nice swim out a distance and then come back and he would sit there while I was swimming and I'd swim for a long time. I think he enjoyed swimming very much, but I think he was always afraid that the last bit of hearing that he had would go if he did very much of it.

Q: All these officers who talk about these afternoons of exercise were not very - they didn't want to be chosen because it would be too strenuous.

Mrs. N.: Yes. Well, you know, there was one incident which I think should be recorded and I only wish that I knew the name of the doctor. Chester must have it. I'm sure Chester must have sent it on to Washington somewhere, but he may not have because he didn't hear of it until while we were living on the island. And this was the story this doctor told him. He said that at this particular time Chester was living on Guam and he, this young doctor, was living - had a place just outside of the main center of the naval section where they had a group of people who had ~~lost their minds~~ mental problems or who were difficult, you see. Battle-fatigue people. And one morning he was awakened very early at 6 o'clock and they said, one of our men has escaped. He said, well get the jeep out and we will start up the road to see if we can find him. Well, they were going along and suddenly they saw coming toward them, running, a man with nothing on but shorts and shoes, and they thought this was their man coming back. He did because he didn't remember the exact man, and all of a sudden, he noticed behind this man running was a jeep with five stars on it and a Marine guard, and just in time he said to his men, "Don't arrest this man." He found that the man they were going after was Fleet Admiral Nimitz taking his morning run.

Q: In his shorts.

Mrs. N.: In his shorts. But Chester was so amused over this. The doctor said he shivered all the way back to think how close he had come to trying to arrest the Fleet Admiral.

(Interruption)

Q: We're going to resume this story now with duty on the Maumee and what followed.

Mrs. N.: Well, when the war broke out the Maumee was sent up to the area around Nova Scotia and, what are those lands up there?

Q: Newfoundland.

Mrs. N.: Newfoundland, to service the destroyers, to give them oil and so forth. And it worked very well indeed. They serviced them at sea and to do it when they were under way and things like this. That worked extremely well, but it wasn't very long after that that they took Chester off the Maumee and sent him as aide - not as aide but he had another position with Admiral S. S. Robison, so he went into submarines again, and then the submarines were very interesting because they went across, he had a chance to go across to Europe. There's one delightful story that - Admiral Robison was a person who just dearly loved to talk to people. He was a very friendly person, and they were at a place in - I think they were having dinner in Belfast, Chester and the Admiral, when some young officers came into the room and they were on the other side of the room, and Admiral Robison spotted them and he said, "Oh, let's go over to talk to these young officers," and he started across the room before Chester could stop him, and these young officers took one look at him, saw him coming, and absolutely vaulted over and fell out of the windows to get away. And he said, "I don't think that's very nice," to Chester and Chester said, "Admiral, they're off limits. They didn't want to see you." They shouldn't be in Belfast. It's against the rules. Chester said it was the most precipitous thing. These submariners took one look and the chairs flew in all directions, and they just dove out of the windows.

Q: Did he run up against Admiral Tommy Hart when he was over there with the submarines?

Mrs. N.: No, I don't think so. Admiral Robison was the

senior one over there and I don't think he ran into...

Q: Hart was a captain.

Mrs. N.: Yes. I don't think he ran up against Tommy Hart. He'd known Tommy Hart for many, many years and we've always been very excellent friends. Of course, I think Tommy Hart is one of the most fabulous people now, at 90 some he's just as lively as ever.

Q: He's one of my dearest friends.

Mrs. N.: He's just absolutely wonderful, and we're just devoted to Mrs. Hart, and we've been up there to see them.

Q: At King House?

Mrs. N.: Yes, at King House, and I get a card from them every Christmas with a lovely message on it. They really are just very good friends of the Nimitz family. I've always wanted to go up and visit them when I was visiting Chester Jr, but it's quite a long ride up to Sharon from New Canaan, and I'm usually there only a day or two and don't have time to go up there.

Q: You know she still rides horseback every day?

Mrs. N. Oh, I'm sure she does. Absolutely delightful. I think my connection with the Harts was particularly at a time when they were very much torn because while I was at the naval hsopital in Oakland, I got word, the doctor came in and said, "They're bringing in young Tommy Hart this afternoon. He's only a few hours to live." And then I got a letter from my husband a day or so afterwards telling about young Tommy standing up to read his orders and falling down with the leukemia, and

I immediately was worried about his little wife and so I said to the doctors, all of whom were good friends of mine, (they were civilian doctors, now in Navy) and I said, "Well, he's only got a few hours to live. Why don't you put a bed in that room with him so that she doesn't have to leave him for the few hours that he's got left?" And they said, yes, they would. Not only did they do that, but the chief surgeon - no, well, one of the men who'd come from Mayo Brothers - I'll think of his name in a minute - had her stay at his house until Tommy got in, and then they let her stay right with Tommy, and these people would take her off when Tommy would be sort of numb to the world, they'd take her up to their house and give her a drink, then bring her back to the hospital. Another young officer, MacCondry, who was out there - no, it wasn't MacCondry it was another one that we were very close to, who gave her his car so that she could run back into town and see her own mother and her little girl and rush back to the hospital. Everybody did everything for her, and then they said that the Harts were coming out, I met the Harts and said, "Stay at my house overnight," and they went out to the hospital to see Tommy and came back and they stayed with me. And I kept saying to them, because I felt that I wanted them to be sure to realize that this little girl that their son had married was really being very wonderful and that she had kept saying to me, "This is going to hurt the Harts so terribly, and I can't do anything about it." He died that night, and I think I had had a chance to talk with the Harts and explain to them how wonderful she had been and they said to me, "Do you really think she meant that?" I said, "I know she did." So they took this little girl and her child back with them to Washington, and she became very close to the Harts and afterward Mrs. Hart said to me one day, "Katherine, I never can thank her enough for what she has done. Through the years she has talked to that little girl about her father until that child has a wonderful idea of her father." And from then on, she spent much time with the Harts and she would come up with the child for Christmas and they would be together with all the other Harts, the rest of the Hart family, and it was very pleasant. And after a great many years, five or six, seven, she married again, and it just meant that she and her new husband and their children and the little Hart girl would come up to the Harts. It was a lovely relationship.

Q: And it continues so. I know them. I know her, I know the daughter, Penny. We were at the 90th birthday party and stayed on for the family dinner and I sat next to Penny. Penny since that time has lost her husband.

Mrs. N.: No. Again?

Q: Yes. The young girl.

Mrs. N.: Oh, you mean the little girl?

Q: Yes. She married and she lost her husband within a year or so.

Mrs. N.: What was it? I mean to say it wasn't in the war?

Q: No. It was in an accident, or something. So that was a

Mrs. Nimitz - 86

very sad thing for them a year ago. And then last year, Isabelle's husband died in a tragic accident.

Mrs. N.: That's right. He was the...

Q: The diplomat. He was electrocuted.

Mrs. N.: Oh, yes.

Q: That was last summer. So they've had a hard time.

Mrs. N.: Well, they've been two staunch people. To some, at times, perhaps he was difficult, very difficult. But he never was difficult with Chester. Chester was very fond of him. Both big Chester and little Chester, because he was in command of the Naval Academy when little Chester was there.

Q: Well, I adore that man. I think he's great.

Mrs. N.: He's a delightful person. We were all amused when he became Senator from Connecticut. It only lasted one term, but I'm sure he brought honor to it, but I'm sure there were lots of politicans that couldn't quite understand Admiral Hart because he probably spoke just as he did in the Navy. Just announced what he was going to do, and announced what ought to be done, and to politicians that isn't exactly the way they want it.

Q: No. it isn't. Shortly afterward you came back and you were at the Naval War College for a brief period. Tell me about the house and the problems of the house there.

Mrs. N.: Well, we came back. You see, we were coming back from Honolulu, from duty - from his duty in the submarine force out there - and our stay there had been very delightful, but just at the end I proceeded to have whooping cough along with the children, and when we got on the transport to come home, there we were with three children, a small Boston bulldog, on a ship in which there was this great discord between the commanding officer and the executive officer. So that the trip to San Francisco was rather interesting and certainly had many enlightening moments. When we got to San Francisco, word came to the Admiral that as we were coming around to the East Coast and as the transport was eventually coming around to the East Coast, would he mind staying on the transport while it was up in Mare Island for overhaul for a while, And trying to re-arrange the schedule of operations on this ship in such a way that there would be more peace, and things would run better. So while he was trying to go over the arrangements for the transport and so forth, we lived on the ship in Mare Island. We had a delightful time. The captain of the ship was very fond of the Nimitzes and the dog and when he went to walk, he'd take the dog, and when we would go ashore we'd take the dog. The children had a wonderful time. Our son wore regulation sailor suits and the sailors would look at him as he would go off the ship and say, "You can't go ashore, your tie isn't properly tied. Go back and get your tie properly tied." Then the Admiral played a great deal of golf up at the Golf Club and we had much fun. When we finally got started around to the East Coast, we felt as if we were plank-owners on the ship having lived there for two months already before we were starting on the East Coast trip down through the Panama Canal. On that trip were several other people who were going to the Naval War College. Among them was Taffinder - Captain Taffinder. He was then a commander, I think. Let's see. No. I guess he was a captain. Anyway, he and the Admiral played - and Captain Bryan, Paddy Bryan - they played innumerable games of cribbage and had a marvelous time doing it.

Q: That was one of the Admiral's favorite games.

Mrs. N.: One of the Admiral's favorite games. I think our children were probably very obnoxious to other children because they certainly had an "in" on the ship that none of the others had, both with the crew and with the mess attendants, you know, and our quarters were quite separate from the quarters of the people coming as passengers on the ship, because they had put us in the section where there were three - we had two rooms and a bath of our own, more or less in the officers' quarters than in the quarters where the passengers were. We got around to Newport and were met by my mother and taken up to Wollaston. And then my husband went back to Newport to hunt for a house and as we got over there rather late and because we have three children, there were great difficulties in finding a house. He finally said he had found a house on Hunter Avenue and it had lots of room, we had lots of room, and it had a big yard...

Q: Was this a stay of a year, or what?

Mrs. N. Yes. Well, it was from June to June, yes. This sounded very nice and for the summer it was very nice. We got down there and the children found a great many friends there, the Crowell boys. Captain and Mrs. Crowell had been on the transport, and the Crowell boys and young Chester were great friends, and some of the girls that were on the transport Catherine knew, so it looked as if it was going to be a wonderful season. And then the trials started. Young Chester developed bronchitis quite badly and had a difficulty in coughing which worried us very much all through the winter, especially as we discovered that this lovely summer house that only three of the eight bedrooms were connected with the furnace, and that there were parts of the house that were just like icebergs all through the winter. After that the fact that there was a coal shortage, and for a house that burned five tons of coal, I think it was, a month, we could only buy it in half-ton lots. So that it seemed to me we were always buying coal, and only soft, powdery coal, so that the danger of explosions when you put it into the furnace were great. Dangers when I used it in the kitchen, in the stove, which I had to do, were also rather great, and the lugging of this stuff up from the cellar to the kitchen was no easy chore. The children had every contagious disease they could think of multiplied by three. By the end of the winter I would have gone anywhere to get out of that area.

Q: This must have been pretty distracting for your husband, who was trying to study...

Mrs. N. No. As a matter of fact, he studied very peacefully. He did most of his studying at the cubby hole they gave him at the War College, and he would read at night, and I remember the morning of his graduation. The children had been taken back to my mother's house in Wollaston, because he had received orders to join Admiral Robison on the West Coast. Admiral Robison was in command of the Pacific Fleet, and the children had gone up to stay with my mother in Wollaston, and we were going to the graduation and, as I remember, turning over, he was reading in the early morning when I woke up, and I looked over at the book he was reading and it said "The Last Engagement of the Battle of Jutland," and I couldn't help but say, "Well, I'm very glad you finally got there," and he turned on me and said very disgustedly, "I have read the Battle of Jutland from beginning to end several times. I was just refreshing my memory." And we went to the graduation and no two people ever left Newport with more joy than we did, because it had been a very hard winter on all of us. We got to New England, got to Massachusetts, my home, and the next day we were to - the trunks were to go off, and we were to leave for California that night, late, by train. My husband had gone to the station, down at the foot of the hill on which we lived, to check the trunks, and my mother's chauffeur was out in the garage and my son was playing with the young boy, much older than he was, who lived next door, and I was upstairs when I heard a shreik from the kitchen, rushed down to see the chauffeur with my young son in his arms bringing him in absolutely unconscious. I called the doctor. Chester came up the hill, we got him, we took the car and we started for the hospital. He had fallen from the

Mrs. Nimitz - 91

roof of the garage next door onto concrete and had a basal fracture of the skull. One side of his head was open a quarter of an inch from top to bottom, inside (2). Needless to say, we did not leave for California that night. The trunks were brought back, and Chester stayed until the child's life - we were sure he was going to live. Then he went on and I was left, and I assure you we looked back on the War College duty and that period just after it as part of our career in the Navy we'd just as soon forget.

Q: Thank you for telling me about it, anyway.

Mrs. N.: Oh, what a day. On the way out, on the transport, the Chaumont, young Chester leaned against the railing to look out, and someone had left a steam pipe uncovered and he went against the steam pipe with his ankle and was fearfully burned. The burn, because he had nothing left to fight with, all of his strength had gone into fighting this other thing, nothing to fight with, and it would not heal. It would crust over and it festered inside, and the doctors would pull the scabs off again. Well I was frantic and when we finally got out to San Pedro I rented a little apartment, one of the kind that used to be there, furnished and it had enough room, and I rented an apartment and went into it. The person who lived in the apartment next to me was a Dr. , I think his name was Houghton, anyway, he was half-Indian, as I remember. He was a Navy doctor and was stationed in San Pedro area, and I would go to the dispensary, come back, and they'd have to pull the scab off again, and it had gotten to where the child was discouraged and I was discouraged, and Dr. Houghton said one day, "I've got an idea. Let's put him to bed in that room where it's sunny. Let's take off all the bandages and everything and just let the sun start working." Inside of a week the leg was healed.

Q: He had to stay in bed?

Mrs. N.: Yes. Stay where he could be with his leg up and let the sun get to him.

Q: How old was young Chester at that time?

Mrs. N.: He was about - well, let's see, that was in '23. He was born in '15. He was about 8 years old. The West Coast finally got him almost cleared up of his terrible cough he had, which he was threatened with tuberculosis at that time, and then, just toward the end of our stay there, he had had one of the first mastoid operations done when we were in - it wasn't Newport - I guess it was New London in the submarine course there during the war. And apparently the doctor had not taken out enough cells and it had been sapping away inside his head, and I happened to be over at the doctor's with Nancy, and this doctor looked at Chester's ear - I said he'd had a mastoid, and he said, "Let me look at it." And he looked absolutely agonized and he said, "Look, bring him back tomorrow if it isn't better." He said, "It isn't draining on the outside, it's draining into his head. You've got to do something and do it quick." So in two days he was in the Long Beach Hospital and they operated on him. They told us he had only a 50 per cent chance of coming through, and poor Chester Sr. had to go to sea with a radio silence the day the operation was performed. He couldn't hear anything. And I spent as much time at the hospital as I could. He had special nurses, and it was a tough go, but he made it, and, of course, long since, had discouraged any idea of his going to the Naval Academy because he was almost stone deaf in one ear. And, do you know, that operation cleaned it out so that he went into the Naval Academy with no problem whatsoever with his ear.

Q: Certainly, he was ill-fated as a child...

Mrs. N.: Oh, he had everything happen. He had basal fracture of the skull, infantile paralysis. He had everything. If he couldn't burst, he broke. He was always having something happen to him, and I guess he still keeps it up. Anyway, he's learned how to handle himself. Let me see what else would be of interest. You know just being around Chester Nimitz was a joy because from the very beginning of our marriage, he never - I have never known him to say, "I want you to do this," he would say, "I suggest it would be nice if you would do this." It was never an order. Neither of us ever said to the other, "Well, I told you so." We always respected each other's opinion, and he'd say, "Well, you know, I think it would be nice if we did this," and he'd wait for my approval, and I would wait for his approval. I think the fact that he was seven years older than I was was a Godsend, because I would probably have been perfectly terribly obnoxious if I'd married someone my own age. I really had a deep respect for the older man that I had married. But he was always so constructive in anything that he suggested, and he was always so thoughtful. Even when he punished the children, he was always so logical about how he did it, and he explained to the children why this was, and why they shouldn't do these things. And I think he was the easiest person to get on with that I can imagine. The easiest person to live with. I think that is one reason that our marriage was so completely happy, was the fact that neither of us tried to boss the other, or to take over from the other...

Q: Important factors.

Mrs. N.: He knew that he was going to be away a lot and that I had to be competent to run finances and all of this, and so I did. It was up to me to pay all the bills, to handle all of those things, and to know what was coming up, what expenses were coming up, to keep track - always when we went to a new place, for the first month, I kept close tabs on all our expenses, until I got a very good idea as to what they were going to be, because we never ran into debt, and we didn't buy an automobile until we felt we could pay for it outright because we didn't want to have to be making payments. The only thing we ever bought that was paid for by the month was, I think, the first washing machine we had.

Q: That was certainly an essential.

Mrs. N.: Oh, it was. When you have many children, there were lots of clothes to wash. I think really to see him with other people, I saw him deal with very difficult people and do it in such a way that they didn't ever realize that they were being dealt with, do you see? They just didn't quite realize

Mrs. Nimitz - 95

except in that how nice he was about all these things and, perhaps, afterwards, they would realize that he was really telling them quite frankly that what they were doing wasn't right and that they'd better change.

Q: They were just gently guided.

Mrs. N.: They were gently guided. All of his younger officers always loved him, and he loved to have them around, and when he had the Augusta going out to China, those officers on that ship would have gone to Hell and high water for him, and they enjoyed so many of the things that he did on the way out. For instance, these were the boys that had just come out of Annapolis. Among them was his future son-in-law, which of course he didn't know at that time. He would stop the ship and then throw out one or two wooden boxes tied together and then he would bring up one of these young officers and say, "You take this ship alongside of those boxes," and the officer would have to turn the ship around and here were these youngsters just like this, you know, never having handled a ship at all. And he would make them bring it up along the boxes that would be in the water. And he'd give them experience in handling ships. On the way out, they all had experience in handling this beautiful cruiser. He did so many things to - he never let them stay, because one officer very successful in one compartment, one particular section of the work on the ship, he would immediately after he became proficient in it, move him to another one, so that each one of them had a chance to work in each department and learn the different departments. He knew those young officers very well by the time he came home.

Q: Kind of a paternal feeling about them.

Mrs. N.: Yes. He felt that they had to be trained and that they must have the best training that he could give them. Then he'd play cribbage with them at night, and they always had a cribbage tournament going, and he just dearly loved them. I remember out in China a delightful incident happened when one of the young officers was Lieutenant Leverton, now the retired Admiral Leverton, and the Admiral was sitting in his cabin - I mean, he was then Captain Nimitz - was sitting in his cabin and he heard taps played so beautifully that he was just terribly impressed and he rushed out on deck to see who had played it. He looked down and there was this young officer of the deck and a sailor standing by, and so forth, and he called over and he said, "Leverton, who was it played taps tonight?" Leverton looked up and laughed and said, "I did." And Chester said, "How did you ever learn to play as beautifully as that?" And he said, "Admiral, as a boy scout I played taps over the tomb of the unknown soldier in Washington." Chester said, "You have a new job. You're to take that bugler we've got and give him some lessons."
When the Admiral had the Augusta and I think he said in some ways that was the happiest duty for him because he enjoyed so much having this beautiful cruiser and traveling through the China Station and to Australia, because he had been on the China Station as a very young officer. When the time came

for him to leave the Augusta, Mary - little Mary, then a child of three - and I went out to the ship, and we had luncheon on the ship and then, after this luncheon, I was taken over by a boat to the SS Lincoln of the President Lines, that we were to come home from China on. The Admiral, then Captain Nimitz, stayed on board and when the time came for him to leave the ship, at the side of the ship was a whaleboat manned by the young officers of the ship, and he was brought over to the Lincoln in this boat, rowed by all the young officers on the ship. And the cheers that they gave him as he went aboard. They dearly loved him, and those young officers, through the years, have come back and back to see us. For instance, Leverton was the Admiral's aide in the Bureau of Navigation. Later on, James Lay became the Admiral's son-in-law. Muddy Waters and Moncure became great friends of ours while we were in Washington. We saw a great deal of them again. All of these people have through the years come back and served with the Admiral in some capacity or other.

Q: That says volumes, too, doesn't it?

Mrs. N.: Yes. I think that that was the cruise that the Admiral dearly loved.

Q: It's always true that a naval officer in his career has one ship that he values more than any other.

Mrs. N.: Yes. This was very delightful because, in the first place, you see, we were at the destroyer base and every plan was for a third year at the destroyer base. I think this was one of the most delightful incidents of the whole thing. We were at the destroyer base and my son was home from the Naval

Mrs. Nimitz - 98

Academy on his plebe leave, and Chester and I were asked out for dinner at a small hotel with Dr. and Mrs. Finnegan. And young Chester had said, don't get the nurse, I'll look out for little Mary, and he and Nancy were left with Mary. We had just finished dinner at the hotel when, sitting in the Finnegans' apartment, when the telephone rang, and Dr, Finnegan said, "Oh, yes. He's right here." My husband went to the phone and we learned afterwards that this was the conversation that took place. My son at the other end of the phone said:

"Dad, how'd you like China?"

Chester said, "Well, I loved it. When I was there I had a wonderful time out on the China Station."

His son, "Well, you'd better like it. You've got telegraphic orders to leave in three days."

Well, this was a bombshell, and when Chester shut the phone off and turned round and told me, my mind was going a mile a minute. I'd just heard that my sister had been operated on for cancer. My baby was named for my mother and mother had never seen her, and I knew that Chester would want to go, and I knew that I would want to go if he went. So, on the way home, our minds were working overtime, and we got back and read the telegram, and that's exactly what it was. We were to start right off. I think they gave us perhaps more than three days, finally. It seemed that Admiral Ingersoll - Captain Ingersoll -...

Q: Was that Royal Ingersoll?

Mrs. N.: Yes...was supposed to take the ship and he didn't

Mrs. Nimitz - 99

want to go out to China, so they were stuck, so they just sent for Chester. So we went out to China.. But it was decided that I go East immediately with little Mary and show her to my mother and see my sister, and Chester, Jr. said, "Mother, I will go East as far as Chicago with you and help you with Mary." Well, this was wonderful, and he was a help, but our problems were many with Mary. Mary had never been in a house. Mary had never lived anywhere but on a ship. Mary thought very lowly of the Southern Pacific train, and she screamed. She cried, she cried, she cried, all the way to Chicago, and I think her midshipman brother who adored her was just very willing to part company with Mary there, while he took the train to Annapolis and I took the one to Boston. I remember I think my son did have a few qualms when he saw his mother starting off in another direction and he knew she would be gone for two years and that he wouldn't be able to come home for leaves. He could go to my family but he couldn't come out to us. We went on to Massachusetts, and then on the way back I was smart and took a whole section and left the top bunk up which made Mary less frightened, and by that time she'd had to live in a house for three days. She wasn't very polite to her grandparents. She was afraid of women. She was used to being handled entirely by the men on the ship. I mean to say that if I was off the ship and Mary wanted to go inside and her nurse happened to be inside, some sailor would pick her up and put her in. So that she was very relieved when we got back to

California, but not a bit happy when she found that we were here in Berkeley living at a small hotel, or boarding house - I guess it was an apartment. Then the Admiral left us there and went up to join his ship, and we went over to San Francisco to live, and they decided to operate on Mary's eyes, one was rather weak, before we went out to China. So we canceled the first ship that we were to go out on and were to take the ship a month later. Mary was very funny on the ship and caused great distress of mind among the passengers because, having lived on a ship all her life, having been taught how to go around the deck of a ship, I was perfectly confident that this little child, who was then just two, and she would go up the ship's steps, up the stairs from the place where our room was, and go out on deck and walk down the deck, and people would start to rush to get her, and Mary became very furious. And they said, "But she's on a ship." I said, "But she's never lived on anything but a ship." If she dropped a toy and it rolled towards the side. Mary always got down on her stomach and went down that way to get the toy, and then back on her stomach until she got well within the...

Q: So she didn't pitch overboard.

Mrs. N.: So she didn't go overboard. And, of course, the deck on the ship going to China had canvas all round it, as it did on the destroyer base. But Mary enjoyed herself on that ship because she was on a ship. But she got out to the Philippines and found she was going to be in an apartment, an old Spanish apartment, and there again, we had great difficulty. She would not take to a Chinese amah. She would go nowhere with her. She would not take to a Philippine amah. The only one she would go out with was the Filipino houseboy, or the boy on the ship who had been on the ship where she was born, or where she had gone to after that.

Q: She was very selective, wasn't she?

Mrs. N.: We had a terrific time for the first part of our cruise because Mary was just not going to be taken care of by a woman, and she didn't want to be ashore. It was a strange life for a little girl and she loved it.

INDEX

for an interview

with

MRS. CHESTER W. NIMITZ

Almsby, Leonore, 75

Aquinas, Mary (Nimitz) 97-101

Arnold, Hap and Mrs., 59

Athletics and exercises, 79-80

Atlantic Submarine Flotilla, 5

Augusta, 95-97

Bassett, Lt. Prentice, 1-5

Berkeley home, 62-64

Bertolet, Commander, 5

Blandy, Admiral W. H. P., 55

Bobby Werntz' School, 8

Bohemian Club, 66-68

Bonds; savings, 45-47

Brahms symphony, 76

Brinser, Harry, 5

Brooklyn, duty in, 31-33

Brüdemann family, 25

Bryan, Captain "Paddy", 88

Canaga, Captain Bruce, 67-68

Carreck, Captain Walter, 55

Chandler, Mrs., 72

Chawmont, 91

Childhood experiences, (Admiral's) 11-15

Chow-Fei, Admiral, 36

CNO: relinquish of, 53-56

Cooley, Mr., 42

Cozard, George E., 77a

Crowell, Captain and family, 89

Daniels, Josephus, 4

de Raguine, Pom, 78

Delbose, 23

Denfeld, Admiral and Mrs. Louis E., 54-55

Derflinger, 24

Diesel engines, 22-24, 34-36

E-1, 2-3

Eching, 20

Eisenhower, Dwight D., 15

Erhmans, Sidney, 77

Estobal, (Nimitz mess boy), 78

Europe; duty in: Hamburg, 22-25; Augsbury, 25-26; Nürnberg, 26-28; Belgium, 29-30

Finnegan, Dr. and Mrs., 98

Fireman rescue, 15-16

First meeting and dates, 1-4

Fore River Shipbuilding Company, 3

Freeman, Miss Elizabeth, 1-4

Glovinavich, Rose, 44

Grady, Henry and family, 77-77a

Greenslade, Admiral John Wills, 49

Griller family, 73-74, 77

Haas, Walter and family, 77-78

Hancock, Joy Bright (see Ofstie)

Hart, Admiral Thomas C. and family, 82-86

Hart, Thomas C. Jr. and family, 83-85

Hearst, Mrs., 72

Henke, Grandfather, 11

Henke, Grandmother, 9-10

Hikayago, Tad, 64

Hinkamp, Lt. Clarence, 3, 5, 15

Hoover, President Herbert, 66

Horton, Mrs. Douglas, 37, 40 (Miss Mildred McAfee)

Ingersoll, Admiral Royal, 98

Jacobs, Admiral Randall, 37

Japanese Terms; signing of in Tokyo Bay, 18-20

Kaiserine Augusta, 22

Keith's Vaudeville Circuit, 3

Kennedy, John F., 20

King, Admiral Ernest J., 44, 49-50

Kloppenberg, 23

Lawrence, John and Edward, 72
Lay, Catherine (Nimitz) 89
Lay, James, 97

Leverton, Admiral Joseph W. Jr., 96-97

SS *Lincoln*, 97

Lusitania, 33

Mare Island, 87

Maumee, duty on, 33, 36, 81-82

McAfee, Miss Mildred (see Horton)

McColough, Admiral and Mrs., 50

McCondry, Commander, 51

McCormick, Admiral Lynn, 49

Moncure, Captain Samuel P., 97

Monteux, Pierre, 74-76

Naval Academy, 8, 15, 97-98; museum, 20-21

Naval War College, 86-91

Nevins, Allan, 17

The New York Times, 78

Newfoundland, duty at, 81

Newport, 88-90

Nimitz, Catherine (see Lay)

Nimitz, Chester Jr., 13-14, 83, 86-87, 89-93, 98-99

Nimitz, Grandfather, 11-13

Nimitz, Grandmother, 13

Nimitz, Mary (see Aquinas)

Nimitz, Nancy, 98

Nonnenbruch, Mr., 25

Oak Knoll; Mrs. Nimitz's service in, 41-42

Oakland Tribune, 44

Ofstie, Mrs. Ralph A. (Joy Bright Hancock) 40

Palmer, Jean, 40

Pauley, Edwin Wendell, 72

Plumley, Congressman Charles Albert, 56

Redman, Admiral John R., 71

Rich, Francis, 40

Robison, Admiral S. S., 82-83, 90

Roosevelt, President Franklin D., 66

St. Alban, Mrs. Margaret, 77

Saltonstall, Senator Leverett, 56

Schiffler, Mr. and Mrs. Kurt C., 55

Sheehy, Father Maurice S., 55

Sheppard, Congressman Harry R., 56

Smith, Paul, 66

USS *South Dakota*, 18

Sproul, Bob and Ida, 72

Spruance, Admiral Raymond Ames, 55, 80

Stern, Mrs. Sigmund, 77-78

Stories, 68-71

Sullivan, Secretary John Lawrence, 55

Taffinder, Captain Sherwoode Ayerst, 88

Tardy, Bill, 5

Texas family introduction, 8-9

Truman, President Harry and Mrs., 57-59

Upton, Dr. John and family, 77

Vandergrift, General A. A., 38-39

USS *Vermont*, 5

Waters, Admiral Odale D., Jr., 97

Waves, 37-40

Wedding, 6-7

West Point, 15

Wiley, Tovah, 40

Woo, Y. C., 20

Interview with Mrs. Chester W. Nimitz

At her apartment, 155 Jackson Street, Apartment 2207,

                San Francisco, California 94111

Subject: Fleet Admiral Chester W. Nimitz

Date: 23 March 1970

By: Professor E. B. Potter

Q: Mrs. Nimitz, I hope this is the last time we'll have to bother you with a recording session. This time, I want to ask you a number of questions. Some you have already answered, so I won't ask them again. I'd like to start by asking you your impression of Anna Henke Nimitz.

Mrs. N.: I was particularly fond of my mother-in-law, whom I consider a very wonderful woman. In the first place, she was a very, very handsome woman, a woman who had had a very hard life, having married my husband's father when she was quite young and then losing her husband before my husband was born. She carried a load, as her second husband, who was the younger brother of Admiral Nimitz's father, was a great talker. He could tell everybody how to do things, but he seemed not too willing to do much, with the result that she worked extremely hard. When I first went down I think they were suspicious of me because I was a Northerner and they weren't quite sure what sort of a person their son was marrying. In the second place, I've always felt that they had sort of picked out a girl down in Kerrville that they would have liked him to marry, so this was a little bit of a jolt, but certainly no one could have been sweeter to me than my mother-in-law. One of the great things that I remember about her, she was a marvelous cook. She had a lovely smile and a lovely laugh. She was very proud and she would not accept invitations from people because she felt that she was in no place to return these obligations, and I can tell you that many of those people said, "Oh, if she would only come to our party we would so love it, but she won't do it because she can't - she feels that she has no money to return these." She had been born, brought up a Lutheran, but when they moved to Kerrville she met a charming Episcopalian minister and his sister named Galbraith and she became an Episcopalian and was extremely happy in that Church. She belonged to their ~~sewing meetings~~, sewing circle, and Dr. Galbraith used to come to the house frequently to call on her. She was, I think - while she did not go out much in the community or have any club life or anything like that... *a much loved member of the community.*

Q: When you went to Kerrville for the first time, were they still running the St. Charles Hotel?

Mrs. N.: Oh, no. They were living in a very tiny little house that didn't even have a bathroom in it, and it was - I think there were about two little bedrooms, a tiny little living room, and a little place to eat off the kitchen, and then there was this enormous yard. The yard was absolutely beautiful in the way of trees - most beautiful trees. There was no particular garden, except Mother Nimitz had a few things

EBP - Mrs. Nimitz - 3

~~out~~ in the way of "animals."

Q: I know where the house was, but it's not there any more.

Mrs. N.: No, it's not there any more.

Q: I'm a little curious to know about the great influence that Admiral Nimitz's grandfather had on him. He seems to have admired him enormously.

Mrs. N.: I think he admired his grandfather because he felt the loss of not having a father of his own, and his grandfather was very fond of this small boy. I think that perhaps, looking back and thinking over the years, I have come to the conclusion that the greatest influence on my husband was from his mother's family, not from his father's, because his mother's family were all terrifically industrious. They all were prosperous because they worked hard, and the Nimitz Hotel where his grandfather lived and - (Chester spent some time with his grandfather,) but the best time with his grandfather Nimitz was when grandfather would take him out on overnight camping trips or a week's camping trip. They would go in a covered wagon with *least two* ~~several~~ horses, and grandfather would always let him take some other small boy with him. They would go out - grandfather would keep the camp and do all the cooking, and these small boys shot their little rifles and did the fishing.

Q: In the Guadalupe River?

Mrs. N.: No, this particular one that I'm thinking of was

EBP - Mrs. Nimitz -4

farther off from the Guadalupe. I have a vague feeling it was in the Llano River. It was the Llano property that was left to my husband by his grandfather - was 99 acres along the Llano River, but my husband was away at the time his grandfather died and one of my grandfather's older sons sold that property without saying anything to my husband. Just sold it and said he was sending him the money, and for 99 acres the money my husband was sent was somewhere around $3,000.

Q: You just said something that puzzles me. You said that Admiral Nimitz's grandfather died when he was at the Naval Academy, but according to all records I can find, he died in 1911.

Mrs. N.: Did he die in 1911? Well, this was before I knew him and I thought it was when he graduated from the Naval Academy that his grandfather died.

Q: No. He died at that time and I have a letter...

Mrs. N.: Well, I thought he died while he was at the Naval Academy. I was wrong. I thought when he went home from the Naval Academy - because - wait a minute, his grandfather - that letter from his grandfather was written to Chester while he was at the Naval Academy.

Q: That's right. Right, on his 17th birthday.

Mrs. N.: Yes, and now he was 16 when he went in, and he graduated at 19, so his grandfather must have been alive while he was at the Naval Academy.

Q: Oh, he was. He died in 1911 after he was out of the Naval Academy...

Mrs. N.: He died just before I met Chester. Well, I'm surprised that that's so because I never heard him speak of his grandfather, except as being dead.

Q: Well, wasn't that the time that he met you? 1911 is when the grandfather died and he wrote it to his mother, "Anything that grandfather left me is yours."

Mrs. N.: Yes, yes. That's it. He did. He gave it to his mother and that is when she bought the little house - in Kerrville, this funny little old place. Later on, with that money and with the money that - I wonder how she got the money for the second? I guess she put some of that money away. Anyway, they built a second little house there and tore down the first one. It was a very simple little bungalow, probably cost around $4,000 or $5,000. I would say not more.

Q: Do you recall whether the Maumee first went to Port Arthur, Texas, on its first voyage?

Mrs. N.: No, not on it's first voyage. It was just on its routine voyages when it would go down to - it went down to pick up oil down in that area, ~~gasoline~~, and it - let's see - the Maumee was - I have to stop and think back now on this. The Maumee's engines were built and he went to sea on it in 1916, it must have been - just before the war.

Q: The Maumee was commissioned in October 1916, and it took its trial runs at the end of December 1916. Now, it doesn't matter if I don't get this here, because I'm going to study the log of the Maumee.

Mrs. N.: Yes. Well, I don't remember just when ~~just~~ whether she went down there for that or not. I know she was down there when I went down there with the two children. It must have been about 1917 or 1918.

Q: I'm just making sure that this figure's up high enough.

Mrs. N.: Yes. Well, either it was '17 ~~or '18~~ that I went down there and saw him down there at that time, because my children were, I think, two and three at the time, and the one that was two would be - yes, it must have been just about 1917 ~~or 1918~~ that I went down there to visit Mother Nimitz and Father Nimitz, stayed a little while with them, and then went on down to Port Arthur when I found that the Maumee was coming in there. I had not expected to see my husband down there.

Q: Do you recall whether Admiral Nimitz - Lieutenant Nimitz, I should say - went directly from the Maumee to the Chicago

EBP - Mrs. Nimitz - 7

in 1917?

Mrs. N.: Yes, he did, because - let's see, he was with Admiral Robison on the Chicago...

Q: That's right.

Mrs. N.: Was it '17 when he went there? Let me see, what are the First World War dates?

Q: We got into the First World War in the spring of 1917.

Mrs. N.: Yes. Then....

Q: And I understand that Admiral Nimitz - Lieutenant Nimitz - went as engineering officer and executive officer of the Maumee and was supplying those first destroyers under Taussig...

Mrs. N.: Yes, he was. I remember how excited he was when he oiled them at sea. That was one of the first experiments with that.

Q: That's how Taussig was able to say we're ready now?

Mrs. N.: Yes.

Q: A very curious thing about that. Joe Taussig, whom I know, is that Joseph Taussig's son, says that his father always insisted that when Sir Lewis Bailey asked that question that he thought he said, "When will you be ready to eat?" and he said, "We're ready now." I don't know whether Joe was joking or not. Where were you living? Were you living in New London when Admiral Nimitz toured Europe with Admiral Robison?

Mrs. N.: Yes. I was living in New London on School Street.

Q: Where was Anna, whom you call Nancy - where was she born?

Mrs. N.: She was born there.

Q: I see. I've asked you...

Mrs. N.: On Sept. 13, 1919, I think it was.

Q: ...this question before, but I want to make sure I have the answer right. What was at Pearl Harbor at the time that you arrived to build the submarine base? What in the way of installations were there?

Mrs. N.: Well, I can't remember. There was the Navy Yard there, where the ships would come in to, but there was - as I remember it - there was nothing where the submarine base was to be, excepting large areas of cactus, which my husband used as disciplinary measures and cleared it in that way. Anybody who was - needed disciplining, he gave them 20 square feet of cactus to clear.

Q: And they had to pull it down with ropes, or something or other.

Mrs. N.: Yes, they had to - and they had to cut it down with machetes and get rid of it.

Q: Did you move to the Rigel when Admiral Nimitz became ComSubDiv 20, Commander of Submarine Division 20?

Mrs. N.: No, no. No, we moved to the Rigel after the submarines.

You see, he had command of Division 20 and at that time we lived up in San Diego in an apartment. Then, when he gave up command of the submarines, we went down to live on the Rigel and he became the commander of the destroyer base, reserve destroyers and others, and we went down there. I can tell you exactly when we went down there, because Mary was born on the 17th of June, we went down there to live on the 16th of June in '31.

Q: Were your quarters in the Rigel comfortable?

Mrs. N.: Very. Very comfortable. They couldn't have been nicer and, you see, we had a good deal of our own furniture, because the other people had taken out their furniture, so we had to - that is to say, I won't say we had a great deal of our furniture, we had some of our dining room furniture in their living room because our living room and dining room were in one. And I think my husband - yes, we had our own bed in our bedroom.

Q: How did you dine there? I mean, did you cook yourself, or ...?

Mrs. N.: Oh, no. We had a staff.

Q: That's what I thought.

Mrs. N.: They had a staff that was a cook and a steward and two mess boys.

Q: I'm having trouble tracing the dwelling places of the Nimitz family while Admiral Nimitz - or Captain Nimitz, Commander Nimits - is aboard the Augusta.

EBP - Mrs. Nimitz - 10

Mrs. N.: Well, of course, the children - one was in the Naval Academy, one was in California, at the University of California. She came out to China to greet us out there - to meet us later on...

Q: That was Catherine?

Mrs. N.: Yes. And Nancy and Mary - Mary was a baby, too, you see - and Nancy was in high school at the time, and we went out to Shanghai - when we were in the Philippines we lived at on Romero ~~Osalid~~ *Salas* in an old Spanish apartment and...

Q: Where is that?

Mrs. N.: It was just off Dewey Boulevard in the Philippines - in Manila. Then, when we went up to China, we tried one or two places first and then we found that the nicest place to live was at the Clement Hotel, which was a Belgian apartment hotel out in the French Concession, and I took an apartment for Mary and myself and the Admiral when he was there, and then the two girls had the apartment next to it, and all we had - there was no cooking, it was a hotel where you ~~go in~~ *went* for meals in the dining room and, incidentally, they were marvelous meals, ~~marvelous meals~~, and with a lovely garden there and the little girl could play, but Mary spent most of her time up at the American School in the afternoon playing in their playground, and Nancy attended the Shanghai American School. Most of the students in the school were American missionaries' children, and they were a smart bunch of cookies, there's no other word.

Nancy really had good competition there, and she still hears occasionally from some of them.

Q: Now, do I have that right? You lived in Manila and in Shanghai?

Mrs. N.: Yes, but we went to Unzen, Jan for the summer.

Q: And then you went off in the...

Mrs. N.: Well, then, you see, ~~when we went up to Pekin~~ when the ship went up to Tsingtao, we went up to Pekin. Then from Pekin, the ship was going up to ~~Shanghai (Chianghai-Kwang?)~~ Shanhaikwan, which is way up in North China, so we went up there and we lived at the hotel of a mining company up there for, I guess it was about a week. I had no amah for Mary. I didn't take my amah with me when I traveled. So every morning I had a mafu and his donkey. They usually loaded coal. They would go out to the ships because it was so shallow there that the merchant ships couldn't bring their coal in very far, so these donkeys would go out at low tide when the ships were just practically on the ground and bring the coal in in sacks on their backs. Well, you can imagine this little donkey thought this was just sheer heaven to have a week off from that and to have nothing more strenuous than to carry a very cunning little girl on its back. And she thought that to carry the little whip with all the thread - all the rope - in it that kept the flies off the donkey's back was just great fun, and of course the donkey thought this was just pure heaven. So the mafu would arrive at 7 o'clock in the morning and sit outside

EBP- Mrs. Nimitz - 12

this little hotel, and when we wanted to go anywhere we simply walked out, put Mary on the donkey's back, and off we would go. We could go walks all through the village and into the country, and Mary just went along on the donkey. And when Mary slept during the afternoon, the donkey slept, and so did his master.

Q: How did she happen to pick up a certain amount of Chinese?

Mrs. N.: Well, Mary didn't pick up Chinese. She spoke - she picked up a little Japanese when we went over to live in Japan.

Q: Oh, you lived in Japan, too?

Mrs. N.: Yes.

Q: In Tokyo?

Mrs. N.: No. We spent a summer, when Chester was on the Augusta ~~he thought~~ they had had word, very secret word from President Roosevelt, that he thought there might be trouble somewhere and he might want the ship to come in to Honolulu to confer with him during the spring. ~~And~~ Tsingtao was a fairly expensive place to stay, and as we had numerous children with college educations coming up, he said, "I don't know whether there's any use in your going up to Tsingtao or not." So, I said, "All right. I'll go over to Japan." So I went over to Japan, and we took a cottage up in Unzen, Japan - a cottage that belonged to some missionaries. There were seven cottages in ~~Kasanukiama~~ KasanoKayama (?), which means the Fairy Glen. To get there after we got off the ship from Shanghai, we took a car at Nagasaki and drove up some 40 miles, up to this mountain place, the road went round many sharp turns. Every time we'd go around a turn there'd be a beautiful waterfall.

Q: This was in Kyushu?

Mrs. N.: Yes, this was on the island of Kyushu. We got up there, and had a very nice, absolutely Japanese house for the summer, and the missionaries had gotten me two maids. One was an amah for Mary, and she was the most charming little soul called Tsurua-san, so she taught Mary Japanese manners, (which pleased one of the Japanese-language students very much)

Q: One reason I bring the language up is that in one of the interviews - I think one of yours - you mention the fact that after you came back to the States she used a ...

Mrs. N.: Oh, yes. Speaking of the Chinese, it wasn't that she spoke Chinese, but she spoke with a Chinese idiom. She spoke English with a Chinese idiom. In other words, she used the sort of expressions you use in China when you're trying to make people - Chinese - understand you, and...

Q: I see.

Mrs. N.: ...and...

Q: Kind of pidgin English?

Mrs. N.: Pidgin English. Well, she objected apparently to these Washington children who'd always led a very secluded life

EBP - Mrs. Nimitz - 14

in this little private school that she was sent to, they laughed at her way of speaking. It was an abrupt - she didn't put in any extra adjectives or anything, and they laughed at her and she would never go back to the school again.

Q: Can you give me the first name of the astronomer, Lerschner, at the University of California? That took over one of Admiral Nimitz's classes when he was in the NROTC?

Mrs. N.: I ought to be able to because - it wouldn't be in that book either. I have a directory, but of course Merschner's.. [Lauschner]

Q: Don't worry. I'll write to the University and find out who he was. Now, I'm trying to get a picture of Admiral Nimitz as Assistant Chief of the Bureau of Navigation. Who were his closest friends during that period of his life? Men friends, particularly?

Mrs. N.: You know, Admiral Nimitz didn't do things outside of his family very much. I would say - he did play tennis. We lived on a street - first, we lived up in Chevy Chase, I don't remember the name of the street, but it was a house that was owned, I think, by David Lawrence. He had built it and he and his mother had lived there. And we gave it up after a year because it had so many trees on it Chester said every bit of his spare time was spent raking leaves in the autumn and he was fed up on it. But, otherwise, we lived near Captain and Mrs. Canega there, we lived near Captain and Mrs. Brian, Paddy Brian, we lived near - oh, there were so many of his classmates around Washington.

Q: I was planning to ask you particularly if he walked to and from work with anybody?

Mrs. N.: Oh, when he walked, he walked with Captain Canaga, and when they rode, one of them would drive ~~either car~~, and Catherine and a young aviator used to ride down to the ~~place~~ *department* with them, and they'd get part way down when suddenly the car would stop and both Captain Canega and Chester would quietly get out and they'd say, "Now you drive the rest of the way. We're going to walk the rest of the way." And this young aviator would take the car over and drive on down *to the department*

Q: I've heard stories of this period when they would try to outdo each other with funny stories to and from.

Mrs. N.: Oh, they really had a marvelous time. Catherine would tell you that, because Catherine was the one that rode with them. ~~Jim, this~~ *The* aviator, used to get a great many laughs out of it.

Q: Why did Admiral Nimitz have only one year's duty on the West Coast between his being Assistant Chief and Chief of the Bureau?

Mrs. N.: Well, that's what we always wondered. We were so pleased to get out of Washington. Well, simply because they just figured that he was the man they wanted there at that time.

Q: And now can you think of anybody he walked with...

Mrs. N.: Because I can assure you he was so pleased to get out on the West Coast and have the battleship division...

Q: I gather Washington wasn't his favorite place?

Mrs. N.: Oh, he would do anything to get out of Washington - both of us would.

Q: Now, did he walk to and fro with anybody when he was Chief of the Bureau of Navigation?

Mrs. N.: Er - well, you see, his children were going back - at least, Catherine and Nancy - no, let's see, when he was Chief of the Bureau of Navigation. No, he usually walked down alone, but he didn't usually have time to walk down very much then. He usually had ~~to take~~ the - ~~let the~~ car take him down.

Q: You told me something on Saturday about Mrs. Gorman. I've gotten some hilarious stories about her, but you gave a very sympathetic picture of her...

Mrs. N.: Mrs. Gorman...

Q: She was the mother of a classmate of his who worked for the Bureau of Navigation?

Mrs. N.: Oh, yes. Well, I have such a distinct picture of the woman. She used to wear her high collar with little bits of bone on each side so that it stayed absolutely straight. She wore clothes - the kind of clothes that were fashionable when she was a girl.

Q: Wear a wig?

EBP - Mrs. Nimitz - 17

Mrs. N.: No. I don;t remember whether she wore a wig or not. I didn't pay that much...

Q: Miss   thinks she wore a wig.

Mrs. N.: Well, she might very well have. But she had on the hats of that same generation. She used to like to wear white when it was summer, and there she was working in the Navy Department, an old woman, and she had high buttoned boots, and I shall never forget seeing her start out, and start across the street, and Oh, I was so scared I thought she was going to be killed because cars were rushing in both directions, and she simply put up her hand, like this, and the brakes screamed and every car stopped, and she walked right across the street.

Q: The stories they tell concern how she'd keep an eye out and if she ever saw the Admiral without a car, she'd come over with a glass of water, or a water glass, and intercept him.

Mrs. N.: Well, he never said much about it, but he did say to me, he said, "You know, it's a tremendous thing for a woman that age to have to go on supporting *herself!*

Q: This next one, you've already answered. It seems that even though the BuNav had shifted to Arlington Annex, his office remained in Washington.

Mrs. N.: Well, Nancy said it shifted at the time he left, just as he was leaving. He didn't want to go over to the

EBP - Mrs. Nimitz - 18

Pentagon, so he was just - they were leaving that office to the end.

Q: Now, I want to get as clearly as possible the story of December the 7th, 1941. The day that we got into the war.

Mrs. N.: When that afternoon, as always, Chester and I went in to turn on the Philharmonic and we were sitting there reading, both of us, and listening to the Philharmonic, and all of a sudden, there was a break and it said, "This is - I've forgotten how they put it on the radio, "This is a break in the program," and they said, "Pearl Harbor has been attacked," and I don't think they any more than got those words out when Chester and I were both up, and he said, "Call Lamar, tell him to get down to the Navy Department. I won't be home till God knows when." And they started.

Q: Did he call Captain Shafroth, or did Captain Shafroth call him?

Mrs. N.: No, Captain Shafroth didn't call him, but Captain Shafroth heard the news and started down. I called Lamar's mother and she said, "He's on his way." She said, "He heard it and he went out of the house like a flash."

Q: But Captain Shafroth did come by and pick up Admiral Nimitz, didn't he?

Mrs. N.: No, he did not. Let's get this straight. Chester went right straight down to the Navy Department. At about an hour or an hour and a half afterwards, the girls and I were

EBP - Mrs. Nimitz - 19

sitting there talking - because, you see, I had Chester Jr.'s wife with me, too, young Chester's because he was out in the Philippines - and, oh, look...

Q: A carrier's passing in front of Mrs. Nimitz's apartment, out toward the Golden Gate. Do you know what carrier that is?

Mrs. N.: That may be the one that they modernized and she's just going out. What is it? The Monterey? No. There's been one that's just been modernized, but there's...

Q: The Franklin Roosevelt, the Midway?

Mrs. N.: No - Midway? It might be, but I don't think that's big enough for the Midway.

Q: We're so used to enormous carriers now that - it's probably quite big. I can't make out the number. I see a 3, but I can't see what else there is.

Mrs. N.: No, well, there is such a common occurrence to me now, to see carriers going in and out, and to see the ships going in and out.

Q: Apparently one of her guns is still - has a capsule over it.

EBP - Mrs. Nimitz - 20

Q: Have you ever heard that they couldn't get to the war plans because it was Sunday? The safe couldn't be unlocked?

EBP - Mrs. Nimitz - 21

Mrs. N.: No. I have not. Of course, you see, that wasn't what was worrying my husband. He wasn't in that section, you see. What he was doing was trying to unscramble who had really been killed and who had not, so that he could notify everybody. So that he could call up all the units that President Roosevelt had said that we mustn't add to the Navy, you know. He would keep saying that, and Chester was doing it on the side. He was bringing in more people all the time, knowing that this was going to happen, and he had - I think I realized that about a week or so before, when the Admiral and I were sitting in the evening, he was reading, studying some papers, and I was sewing and sitting on the couch, and I suddenly looked up and he was looking at me as if he wanted to carry the picture with him.

Q: When was this?

Mrs. N.: This was just about a week before this thing came off.

Q: Did you ever go to the White House when President Roosevelt was president?

Mrs. N.: Oh, yes.

Q: How did Admiral Nimitz think of President Roosevelt?

Mrs. N.: I can't tell you. I think that - I really have the feeling in my heart that Admiral Nimitz felt that the great one in that family was Mrs. Roosevelt.

Q: Somebody said that he felt that President Roosevelt was a bit theatrical in his manner.

Mrs. N.: Well, I think that Chester would feel that way, I think a little bit. Chester was so simple himself.

Q: Have you any memories of what he told you of the days that followed?

Mrs. N.: Well, the days that followed - he would come home perhaps one o'clock in the morning and get just a few hours' sleep and go back.

Q: But he was called into conferences with the Secretary of the Navy and the CNO from time to time...?

Mrs. N.: Well, I do not know that because I had a good deal to think of because I had Joan there, and Joan at that time was expecting another baby in a few months, and her husband was right in - was depth bombed, you see, on the same day out in the Philippines Dec. 7th or 8th

Q: Oh, yes.

Mrs. N.: But he got out of it.

Q: He had a submarine then?

Mrs. N.: He was not in command. He was the third officer on a submarine. But I had a great deal to think about. There was my own family, and he didn't do much talking when he came home. He was too tired. He wanted to get away from it. But he - the night - it was about four or five nights after Pearl

Harbor when everything was all stewed up and - he came home - I had stayed in bed that day because I had a runny cold, and I thought, I'll get over it in one day if I take it now - and I was lying there sort of relaxing in bed, and he came into the room and he sat down by me, and he didn't say very much and he kept looking at me. Finally he said, "Have you got a fever?" And I said, "No, Sweetheart, what is it? What's happened?" And he looked at me with the most tragic look in his face, and he said, "I'm to be the new Commander-in-Chief of the Pacific." And I said, "Well, darling, you always wanted command..."

Q: What time was that of the day?

Mrs. N.: It was in the evening, about 6 o'clock.

Q: Of the 17th, that would be, wouldn't it? The 17th of December, I believe?

Mrs. N.: Let's see. It was about - yes, it was just about then, the 17th, and I said, "You always wanted to command the Pacific Fleet. You always thought that would be the heighth of glory." And he said, "Darling, the fleet's at the bottom of the sea. Nobody must know that here, but I've got to tell you." And I said, "If there's anyone in the world that can save us, you can." And he said, "I hope so." Well, I got right up, got dressed, I went out and had supper with them all, then went down to the basement...

Q: Had supper with...?

Mrs. N.: With Chester and with Catherine and Joan and Nancy. and, and little &

Q: I see, with them all?

Mrs. N.: Yes, well, because the children always had dinner - had their meals with us. And we sat there talking, and after supper I went down into the basement - we had a very disagreeable old janitor - and I said, "Get me up this and this and this, right now. Not tomorrow. Now." And I got Chester's things up there and I said, "Now, what are you going to want?" And he told me what. He said, "I won't need any blue clothes because I'll be out in the tropics."

Q: He said he got packing and he was so confused that he was packing his tuxedo.

Mrs. N.: Well, he - no, well, he didn't pack. I packed up his white clothes he said he wanted and his khakis, and I didn't put in his blue things because he told me not to. So that, later on, he sent for them, he said he might have to go where it was cold. He might be going   , he thought, and ? so I had to send his blue things out. Then I got the blue uniform all packed and went down to mail it and the postman said to me, "You can't send that box." And I said, "Why not?" He said, "It's too big." I said, "Look, do you see who this is going to?" He said, "It cannot be sent." So I called the Navy Department, and the Navy Department called back and said to this postman, "It can be sent, and anything else he orders can be sent." Chester himself had put in the limit of sizes that were to go to the Pacific, and then of course this was much bigger. Anyway, it went off safely and it got there. The very last morning, of course, he went up to Mary's school to a play.

Q: Yes, he mentioned that in his interview.

Mrs. N.: Yes, and it was very sweet.

Q: What school was that?

Mrs. N.: Well, it was the public school in Washington that is on - it was on Q Street. You see, Mary had gone to the Quaker School the first year we were there, and I've never seen such undisciplined children in my life. We had them all to a party and they nearly disrupted the household, and I said Mary goes to public school next year. The following year we'd had a party with Mary and with these public school children, the butcher's child, the delicatessen people's child, and so forth, and I've never seen such sweet, beautifully brought up children - manners galore, and, of course, this was a great thing for them because Chester had just been named Commander-in-Chief of the Pacific, or, rather, Commander of the Pacific Fleet, and while the thing was going on, I think it was Admiral Shafroth sent her a singing telegram, "Happy Birthday," and the children thought this was just too marvelous for words, to see this young boy coming in singing "Happy Birthday". It was a very pleasant occasion.

Q: When was this "Happy Birthday" telegram?

Mrs. N.: This "Happy Birthday" was sent the following - you

EBP - Mrs. Nimitz - 26

1942

see, in February - I don't mean February, in June of that year, after Chester had gone.

Q: Whose birthday was it?

Mrs. N.: Mary's birthday.

Q: I see. Now, I'm trying to get this story - he goes to the school to see the Christmas play...

Mrs. N.: Oh, he went to the school to see the Christmas play and then he came home, and we were all there together for luncheon, and he was to leave about 2 o'clock, and he was in civilian clothes, you see, because...

Q: He took your maiden name?

Mrs. N.: Yes. And LaMar was in civilian clothes. LaMar was to go to the West Coast with him.

Q: Why did LaMar pick the name Wainwright? Didn't he pick the name Wainwright?

Mrs. N.: Just picking a name.

Q: He took his wife's maiden name? No, he wasn't married, that's right.

Mrs. N.: No, I don't know why he took the name Wainwright, unless it was his mother's name. We all sat around and talked. LaMar sat there for a while talking to the girls and Chester and myself, and then LaMar very tactfully said, "I'm going down and wait in the car." And he went down and the rest of us stood there. No time - there's a destroyer going out.

Q: A destroyer's now passing in front of the apartment. A wonderful sight from this window, Mrs. Nimitz's front window.

Mrs. N.: LaMar went down and the girls and Chester and I talked. At no time did I break down, ~~at any time~~. I was brought up by my mother, you take what's coming and you don't weep over it. You have to go through things. It was very sweet because when he left it was just as if he was going off for the day.

Q: Did you go to the station with him?

Mrs. N.: No, because they didn't want anyone to be recognized, you see. They wanted him to be alone. So I didnot go to the station. None of us went to the station, and he went to the station and went right aboard his train and they pulled out. The story of that trip across the Continent, ~~which~~ you probably have, which is very funny indeed. We went right on as if we had to carry on with whatever we were doing. But the children immediately - immediately we said goodbye to Chester the children did not come back into the apartment, they went into their apartment and I went into mine.

Q: At what point did LaMar leave Admiral Nimitz? San Francisco, I think.

Mrs. N.: No. He left in Los Angeles. They didn't come in to San Francisco. They went in to Los Angeles.

Q: Oh, I see. Then the train goes down to San Diego.

Mrs. N.: ~~Yes. Then,~~ No, Somebody met Chester in Los Angeles.

Q: Do you know who met him?

Mrs. N.: No, I don't remember.

Q: Captain Anderson.

Mrs. N.: Was it Captain Anderson? Well, I know that he went down. by car.

Q: That's where they first met.

Mrs. N.: And he stayed with Gunther, with Admiral Gunther on the air station, and Gunther and Mrs. Gunther, of course - Mrs. Gunther's here now, she's a great friend of mine - and they felt very concerned over Chester, and they wouldn't let him go out. You see he was held up several days because there was a terrible storm and they wouldn't let him go, and - it's just like Captain Sherman. Forrest used to say, we'd be flying somewhere, and Forrest would cancel the flight and say, no, we can't go on tonight. Chester'd say, why not, and he'd say, "Well, if you're valuable enough to be the Commander-in-Chief, you're too valuable to take a chance on this storm, and we're not flying tonight."

Q: There's a question I would like to ask and may be I shouldn't. Don't answer it unless you want to. But would you say that the Freemans were people in comfortable circumstances at the time that you got married?

Mrs. N.: I can tell you quite frankly. My grandfather was known as - the place they lived on down at Wellfleet, there was another sea captain lived opposite them, and it was known as Money Hill. My grandfather started the first bank in the town, and grandfather was an excellent businessman, and he was supposed to be a very wealthy man as money went in that time. It was nothing to what money is today. But when he turned it over to my father, there was a question of whether to sit in an office and charter ships or play golf. Golf won. And I can assure you that the Freeman family were not an affluent family, although afterwards, after we were married in 1913 and the war started, you see. Then shipping became very important, and father was willing to send his schooners over into some of the areas that were ~~taking chances on them~~ dangerous, so that - oh, there was a time afterwards when they had a chauffeur and kept two maids and so forth and so on. Father always went through everything he got just as fast as he got it. He lived beautifully when he had it. He had a good time.

Q: Are you getting tired, Mrs. Nimitz?

Mrs. N.: No, not a bit. And he still played a great deal of golf, so he ended up without anything. He left not a cent, but ...

Q: Now, my next question you may not know. I haven't asked you much about the World War II period because you weren't out there, but do you know whether having experienced officers like Admirals Theobald, Block, and Pye made things easier for

Admiral Nimitz during his first days at Pearl Harbor?

Mrs. N.: Having those particular people there?

Q: They were - well, Admiral Block was there, had been CinCUS and CinCPac before Admiral Richardson was.

Mrs. N.: I know. He was a little resentful, I think. Of course, they couldn't help but be. Here was this man 21 down the list suddenly shoved up there. It was sort of a - but Chester was so tactful, and you know he never - he always tried to smooth everything over and make things as pleasant - I don't really remember very much about it.

Q: Do you know when Admiral Nimitz visited the White House during World War II?

Mrs. N.: Yes, we went - the only time - I went back with him both times that he went and the first time, Knox met us and I think he went to call on the President the next day for just a short time. And the second time...

Q: You don't recall about the time that - what year that was?

Mrs. N.: Let's see - it must have been - the second time was in 1945 because Catherine suddenly decided she wanted to get married while we were there.

Q: Oh, well, that was in October 1945?

Mrs. N.: Yes.

Q: During the war he visited the White House, I don't know quite what time. I think it must have been in the late spring of 1944.

Mrs. N.: I would say '44. Not before that.

Q: Do you know if he met with Winston Churchill?

Mrs. N.: I can tell you he did not meet Winston Churchill at any time until after we were back there in the CNO house.

Q: The reason I ask this - I'm puzzled. You know, the second doctor who lived with him was Dr. Anderson?

Mrs. N.: Yes.

Q: And he brought back Dr. Anderson a Churchill cigar back.

Mrs. N.: Yes, but it wasn't because he met Churchill.

Q: That's why I was puzzled.

Mrs. N.: No, because I can tell you when he met Churchill. When we were at the CNO - oh, it's a great English name - anyway this woman's husband was Minister from England at the time. He was No. 2 to the ambassador, and the ambassador was away, and she called up and said to me, "Mrs. Nimitz, Winston Churchill has just arrived in town from Florida, where he's been vacationing, and he wants very much to talk to your husband, and he wants very much to meet your husband. He's never had the privilege. I asked him who he wanted to meet and he said, just Admiral Nimitz. I want to meet Admiral Nimitz. Can you arrange so that I can?" And she said, "Will you come to dinner tonight?" And I said, "Well, this is a problem because we were going to dine somewhere else." And I said I'd call Admiral Nimitz because I know Admiral Nimitz wants above everything to meet Winston Churchill." So I called up and explained to the people that we were going to dine with, and they said that's perfectly all right. So, we went to this dinner and Admiral Nimitz was delighted to meet Winston Churchill and it was quite obvious that Winston Churchill was delighted to meet Admiral Nimitz, and after dinner - there were only about six of us at the table, I think. Because Winston Churchill said, I don't want a dinner party because I want to [to] Nimitz. So, after dinner, they went in and Churchill smoked his terrific cigars and drank his brandy and soda, and then he took Chester aside and they sat down and Winston Churchill said to him, "What was your lowest point in the war?" And then he told Chester what his lowest point in the war was, and they talked, they just never said very much more about it, but they had a wonderful talk together that evening, and they must have talked for an hour, an hour and a half there.

Q: Going back to '44, did Admiral Nimitz take dinner at the White House?

Mrs. N.: No, I don't think so. No, I'm sure he didn't.

Q: I want to put a story in at this point which was preserved, about when President Roosevelt asked him why he went on and hit the Marianas after the raid in Truk, or rather he sent Admiral Spruance to do that, and he told the story about the famous surgeon, you know, who was to operate on the old man and the old man had a sore throat. I wanted to bring that in at that time.

Mrs. N.: Yes.

Q: Now, next. Oh, yes, the other day you said something that I hadn't heard before. You told me about the long sleep of Admiral Nimitz after the Battle of Midway.

Mrs. N.: Yes.

Q: Do you remember anything else he said about those days?

Mrs. N.: Well, he told me once, he said, "You know, I was just about ready to think they'd better put somebody in because I found I was staying awake day and night trying to figure this thing out," (and he looked like the wrath of God.) I have one or two pictures of him, or rather, I had, I think they're back at Catherine's now, where he looked just drawn through a knothole. And then he said, "After the Battle of Midway" - and he kept writing me in his letters saying "Before long, something will happen," and he was so tired and he was so sure that he had it in the bag, so to speak, after Midway, having all those carriers down and having what he considered even more important than the carriers, was the fact that the fliers were killed. They couldn't train those again in a hurry.

Q: Perfectly true.

Mrs. N.: And he knew then that he had 'em licked, and the relief was so great...

Q: He had no reason to expect a victory before that battle. No. reason.

Mrs. N.: No, no.

Q: And yet - pardon me, if I call him Bill [LEVERTON?] every now and then, but it comes and goes in the interviews so that I've got used to speaking of him in that way - passed through not long before the battle and he said the Admiral took him into the plot toom and told him, this is how we're going to get those Japanese, as if he were perfectly confident that the victory was coming.

Mrs. N.: Yes, yes. He was - you know, this is just Chester's - Chester left nothing to chance, so to speak. In other words, when other people were playing bridge at night or having a good time, he was reading, he was studying. I don't think there was a campaign anywhere in the world from Julius Caesar on that Chester Nimitz hadn't read and studied, day and night. All the mistakes of the Battle of Jutland and all of those things over there, he knew those and he knew all the little islands of the Pacific. He had studied every little island.

Q: I recall one time, we went to the waterfront here in San Francisco and he said, "I want you to see this. What do you see out there. You see the horizon." And I said, "No, I don't. It blends into the sea because there a mist lying over it." That's the way it looked during the Battle of Jutland, and that's why they couldn't get the fix.

Mrs. N.: Yes, well this is just it, and Chester, I think,

after, when the Midway battle was over and he went in there, that was the 24 hours that he had to have to sleep. And he told Morgan Watt about it, because you see the Watts used to be with us a great deal, and Morgan - this interested Morgan, he's put it down several times, how the Admiral said he just - they were shaking him awake. They thought he had died.

Q: One very interesting picture, Admiral Layton said that when the news came in that convinced them that at least three Japanese carriers were put out of commission and that we had a good chance of a victory, the Admiral's eyes - talk about blue glow. Do you recall his reaction to the sinking of the four heavy cruisers at the Battle of Savo Island? Did he say anything about that?

Mrs. N.: He was very upset over it.

Q: Of course.

Mrs. N.: Very upset over it. But, you know, he didn't talk too much. He just told m e, he said, "This shouldn't have happened," but he was very careful about making any comments.

Q: Yes. As a matter of fact, his dsicretion makes it very hard to get the story sometimes.

Mrs. N.: Well, as he said, he's always said, it's human to make a mistake, he said, and we have to - that same person may do a wonderful job later.

Q: Well, as a matter of fact, look at what Admiral Turner did do, and Admiral Turner was partly at fault there.

Mrs. N.: Yes. Well, the Admiral would be - he was a person who tried only to say just the nice things about people, and shut up on the others.

Q: I'm not trying to build a controversy, I'm thinking how he reacted as much as possible.

Mrs. N.: No. Oh, well...

Q: It was a marvelous thing the way he concealed his anxiety before the Battle of Midway.

Mrs. N.: Yes, yes. I used to get it in my letters.

Q: I imagine you did. Did you ever hear of Secretary Forrestal trying to relieve Admiral Nimitz toward the end of World War II?

Mrs. N.: Not - no, he didn't try to relieve him, but what he wanted - he didn't want him to be CNO.

Q: I know that, but even during the war something came up there...

Mrs. N.: No. I think that perhaps at one time he thought he could get Towers out there, but I don't think - then Towers got in the trouble around - I mean to say he made difficulty in Washington and Admiral King got rid of him. He sent him out because Chester said he could look out for him.

Q: Somebody has said something of the sort. I can't think who it is now, and there was the case of Mr. Pauley coming out

EBP - Mrs. Nimitz - 37

there and...

Mrs. N.: I've never heard that in this world. <u>Never</u>, and Chester usually told me most of these things in the background.

Q: I was sorry I didn't get to see Mr. Pauley. Our representative out here will see him, but he just gotten back from New York and just couldn't see me that day. Well, you've already answered 44. What was Admiral Nimitz's opinion of Admiral Towers?

Mrs. N.: Well, Admiral Nimitz said he was very good in the job Chester put him into, but he was not - Chester did not admire people who had disagreeable dispositions or who - I think that my husband had little patience with people of that nature.

Q: His comment was that "I didn't like his way of doing business."

Mrs. N.: No, that's exactly it.

Q: Are you tired?

Mrs. N.: No, no. I can go on all day.

Q: Let's see. A list, in order, of the cities visited by you with Admiral Nimitz in October 1945, after the signing of the - I think you went first to Washington, didn't you?

Mrs. N.: We went first to Washington...

Q: Now, you met him first here in San Francisco, didn't you?

EBP - Mrs. Nimitz - 38

Mrs. N.: Yes. I met him in San Francisco here, and San Francisco wanted so badly to have a big celebration. Then, you know, Washington said you cannot do it, and San Francisco was furious because this was where Chester - where I had been where I'd worked all through the war, and they wanted to have a big party, and Washington said, you cannot do one thing for him, but they did, they had a little luncheon of very fine people here in San Francisco. We did have that luncheon, and then of course he came - and we had a ride up the street, just so that people could see him. But we took the plane that afternoon for Washington, and then at Washington we stayed outside of Washington, at I guess it must have been Patuxent or some place like that, that night, and then went in on the plane.

Q: Then, was it during that visit - this is Nimitz Day in Washington, October the 5th, I believe it was?

Mrs. N.: Yes.

Q: During this visit - was it during this visit that Admiral Nimitz told Secretary Forrestal that he wanted to be CNO?

Mrs. N.: Oh, no. It was before that. It was when we - it was when he came back just at the end of the war - I guess in October.

Q: Well, October, the war was over now.

Mrs. N.: Yes. I mean to say - well, you see, he was still out there on the fleet though.

Q: What I mean to say, he signed the peace document in early September.

Mrs. N.: Yes, I know.

Q: Now, he's come back and he has Nimitz Day in Washington.

Mrs. N.: Yes, but before we went on to Nimitz Day, I think he was - I think we went on - he came back and we went on there and, of course, King was still Commander-in-Chief and King was fighting for Chester all down the line.

Q: I know that. Who was it that Forrestal had in mind to be CNO?

Mrs. N.: Oh, this is - I'll tell you who it was. It was Edwards.

Q: I thought President Truman wanted Edwards.

Edwards had had one heart attack at the time and was also - had been in Washington all through the war. He had not been out in the Pacific or out in the Atlantic at all, and it was after he'd been made CNO that Edwards felt he had to come and call - Edwards and Mrs. Edwards. And I could just see that they were just very unhappy, because she practically told - the word had gotten out that he was going to be CNO you see, and then they weren't. No, President Truman was the one that gave Chester the appointment.

Q: Oh, I know he did, yes.

Mrs. N.: And, was he grateful he did because he certainly thought that the sun rose and set in Chester.

Q: Now, after Washington, you go to New York, is that right?

Mrs. N.: Yes, I think New York was the next one, and from New York we went back to Washington, then we went down to the Texas one.

Q: Now, which city did you visit first in Texas? Fredericksburg or Kerrville?

Mrs. N.: The first one we visited in Texas was Austin. We landed in Austin, and then we went up to Fredericksburg, but at Fredericksburg we didn't go into the town to see anybody. At Fredericksburg we picked up the buckboard or whatever this thing was, this great big, more like a stage, and took that, drove over to Kerrville because that took all the morning to drive that distance.

EBP - Mrs. Nimitz - 41

Q: So you didn;t go to Fredericksburg first?

Mrs. N.: Not - the Fredericksburg came in the afternoon. We went back to Fredericksburg for the afternoon entertainment and for the dinner.

Q: The coach then goes over to Kerrville and you met at the county line?

Mrs. N.: No, well we met - we met them, yes, just at the county line isn't very far, and Governor Coke Stevenson was driving, Chester was sitting beside him, Sherman and I were in the next seat and in the back one was Min Miller and LaMar.

Q: Now, did the Admiral get his high school diploma at the high school?

Mrs. N.: No, he got it at the field where we were.

Q: And it was given by his old principal, Mr. Tolan?

Mrs. N.: Yes, Mr. Tolan.

Q: I brought something to show you. How much education did you say Admiral Nimitz had had before he went to the Naval Academy?

Mrs. N.: He told me that he went to school when he was about 8, and he went into the Naval Academy when he was just 16. When he went to school he had always spoken German.

Q: You said there was somebody whom we must bring out in this biography?

Mrs. N.: And that is Miss Susan Moore.

Q: I've seen her picture.

Mrs. N.: Yes. You have the thing he wrote about her?

Q: Yes, I have the article he wrote for Boys' Life?

Mrs. N.: Yes.

Q: Yes, I have that.

Mrs. N.: Well, this - she was a wonderful woman, and when we went down there when we were first married, he said to me "One person I want you to meet is Susan Moore." And we drove - we rode out in the country, we were both riding, and here was this maiden lady, out there, and she was thrilled to see Chester. She was what in New England we called a "sparse" lady. There wasn't an ounce of any extra flesh on her, but with a marvelous face, a marvelous sense of humor, and a magnificent teacher of mathematics.

Q: I bet she was.

Mrs. N.: Chester really dearly loved her and he wrote to her once or twice, and in the last years of her life when she must have been about 80-some or 90, her sister died, and she married her sister's husband, so that she died a married woman after many years of having taught the children of the country thereabouts.

Q: Isn't that interesting? Did you visit the White House

during the time that you lived at the CNO house?

Mrs. N.: Oh, frequently. And Mrs. Truman and I had lots of fun because we had a lot of jokes together, and I would - we would seek each other out quite frequently to sit together so that she could hear the jokes.

Q: What was Admiral Nimitz's actual feeling about being relieved as CNO after two years? Was he glad to leave?

Mrs. N.: I think he was very glad to leave because he was a very tired man. Do you realize he had had no leave, no leave for six years? They gave him one leave during - I mean, he could have taken, he did take one leave during the time he was in the CNO, and I must say I couldn't get him back there fast enough. He was impossible! *Too restless!*

Q: You have already answered this,- but I would like to get it on the tape. Why did Admiral Nimitz decline President Truman's request that he again become CNO?

Mrs. N.: Simply because he felt that that should not be. There were other people coming up that were qualified and that to recall him was stopping some officer from the chance of being top man in the Navy, and therefore he told the President that he would be - he said, "If you order me back, I will go willingly, but I feel that you should not break the chain of command, that you should go down rather than go back."

Q: And where were you when Secretary Matthews called on you?

Mrs. N.: He did not call on us. He sent word that he wanted

EBP – Mrs. Nimitz 44

to see Chester, and he said, "I want to see you and I will be at such-and-such a hotel," I don't remember what the hotel was, in New York tomorrow, and I want to see you."

Q: And Admiral Nimitz went to his hotel?

Mrs. N.: And Admiral Nimitz went to the hotel.

Q: Were you living at the Claremont [~~Fairmount~~] when Admiral Nimitz joined the Bohemian Club?

Mrs. N.: No. I was living in our house in Berkeley.

Q: Oh, as late as that, was it?

Mrs. N.: Yes.

Q: Oh. When did you move to the Claremont [~~Fairmount~~]?

Mrs. N.: We were at the Claremont in - just when we came up from San Diego and were waiting to find a house. We were there just for a short time - three or four weeks.

Q: When did Admiral Nimitz become regent of the University of California?

Mrs. N.: I think we arrived in San Diego at my daughter's house one afternoon and I think within two days we had the telegram from Earl Warren asking ~~if~~ my husband if he would become a regent of the University. *Dec. 1947 or Jan. 1948*

Q: Do you recall what year that was?

Mrs. N.: Yes, very well. When were the twins born? Wait a

minute. It must have been '47 because it was when we left the Navy Department.

Q: You have confirmed that...

Mrs. N.: Oh, it was the very end of '47 or the very first two days of '48.

Q: That's close enough. You confirmed that Long View was purchased in June 1948. Now I want to get the story of the Griller Quartet. When did you meet these people?

Mrs. N.: After we had been at Long View for a short time, our son came out to be the executive officer of the Naval ROTC at the University of California, and our son was a great devotee of music and played the violin. And he came out one day and he said, "God, what a wonderful time I've had. Yesterday, I went up to listen to the Griller Quartet practice at the University of California in their music room. I've never heard such music." He went back and he wrote a note to Sidney Griller, telling him how much he had enjoyed it.

Q: Would you name all four members?

Mrs. N.: Yes. There was Sidney Griller, there was Philip Burton - no, wait a minute, yes, Philip Burton...

Q: Any kin?

Mrs. N.: No. Philip Burton - not to my knowledge. Jack - this is awful.

It doesn't matter.

EBP - Mrs. Nimitz - 46

Mrs. N.: Oh, wait a minute. I have it right here. I'll give it to you in a minute. Then, the other one was Colin Hampton. He was the cellist.

Q: I got the impression it was a family quartet. Now I see different.

Mrs. N.: No. It was not a family guartet, but they had played together for 25 years, and they had been, during the war, over in England. They used to play to all the camps and so forth and they were decorated by the Queen - Sidney was decorated by the Queen of England for his contribuation.

Q: And Sidney was first violinist?

Mrs. N.: Sidney was first violinist.

Q: It would be marvelous if you remembered all these names after so long.

Mrs. N.: I'll give it to you in just one second - oh, I'm so ashamed of myself. I know Jack so well. They were at the house practically all the time. In fact, I had a lovely large living room and William Primrose was going to play with them, make a fifth. They came to the house to practice.

Q: (We went to get a book, and now we'll resume.)

Mrs. N.: Well, we'll find the Griller Quartet because they're all around here. The Grillers came to live within a block of us, and we saw a great deal of them.

Q: That was Sidney, his wife, Honor, and the little girl, Catherine?

Mrs. N. The little girl, Catherine. Incidentally, Catherine is an actress in England now. Her husband won a large prize for the BBC and he is now one of the best-known playwrights in England. Catherine as a little girl - the Grillers would have to go away frequently - and she resented the people her mother left at the house to look after her, so she discovered that her beloved Admiral and his wife loved to have her at his house, so she would come on down and say, "Mother and Daddy have to go away. Can I stay with you?" And she would come and spend several days with us. And among the other things that she discovered was that Admiral Nimitz was an expert...

Q: With zippers?

Mrs. N.: With zippers. So that she used to come - now, here again, let's see if I've got - this is so funny. Here's Dame Myra Hess and all of that. Now let's see, he must be here somewhere. Catherine Griller, Honor Griller - no.

Q: You were speaking of the night the Griller Quartet played?

Mrs. N.: They were going to play one of Block's quartets, and Block's quartets were quite modern, and before the intermission in the concert, they played this Block quartet, and the Admiral sat through it with grace but with not enjoyment. Then he looked at the program, and saw that they were going to repeat - the Block number afterwards, and while they were out at the intermission and everybody was walking around, Chester

EBP - Mrs. Nimitz - 48

walked up and put a slip of paper on Sidney's ~~thing~~ violin case, "One Block, fine. Two Blocks too many."

Q: Do you recall if Admiral Nimitz liked Shostakovich?

Mrs. N.: Yes, he did. He enjoyed him, but not particularly. The Admiral enjoyed - he was very fond of Brahms and Beethoven and wasn't so fond of Shostakovich, except for Peter and the Wolf - was that Shostakovich, no it was not.

Q: ~~Procopius~~. PROKOFIEV

Mrs. N.: It was ~~Procopius~~ PROKOFIEV that wrote Peter and the Wolf, that was it. He loved Peter and the Wolf.

Q: The reason I mentioned Shostakovich - that concert that you listened to on December the 7th began with Shostakovich, and then went into a Brahms concerto.

Mrs. N.: Yes. Well, ~~no...~~

Q: Did you know that the people who were actually hearing that music were informed of the attack when the whole program was over?

Mrs. N.: Well, I think it's probably just as well they weren't, because I can imagine...

Q: I checked that with The New York Times.

Mrs. N.: Here's Bruce Canega's signature. Oh, how fond Chester was of that man. He was such a sweet person, and here's Bruce Canega, Margaret Canega, Bruce Canega and Elizabeth Canega.

Elizabeth Canega is dying right now. She's very ill. Her sister called me up the week before last.

Q: What I want to know now is when you met the Hungarian Bata [Batha] girls?

Mrs. N.: We met them when Mary was a senior at the convent.

Q: That would be?

Mrs. N.: She was a senior - well, she graduated from Stanford in '53. It must have been around '49. We were at the United Nations. Nancy was living in our house, and Nancy went over to get Mary for Easter vacation, and Mary said to her, "Nancy, there are four Hungarian girls here who are here on scholarships. They have no money to go anywhere and they haven't any friends around here. Couldn't we take them home with us?" And Nancy said, "Why, of course. I'll ask Mother Margaret." So she asked Mother Margaret and she said, "Oh, I'd be so grateful to have those girls to have some place to go." So Nancy took the four of them home, and she wrote later on and said, "I've never known five such willing pairs of hands as I have..."

Q: Did the Bata girls live at your house after you came back to Long View?

Mrs. N.: They didn't live there, but they'd come home for weekends, and they'd spend the Christmas vacation there, and Thanksgiving they were there, and whenever they wanted to be there. And occasionally Mary would call up and say - of course,

Mary went to Stanford the next year - but she went over to see someone at the convent and called me one day to say, "Mother, I think Marta is very sick. I think you'd better go over and see her." And I got over there and Mother Margaret was terribly concerned. It was a question of - the girl not only had 'flu...

Q: They were living in the school?

Mrs. N.: They were living in the school, but the girl had problems that were worrying her mentally terribly. She was the youngest one. She'd been pulled out when she was very young. So I remember Chester and I took her home - I took her home, I took her right back with me and I called Chester and told him that she was sick, to get the guest room ready, and that I'd bring her back. She wasn't as young as I say, because she was in - at that time, she was a freshman or a sophomore in high school. Anyway, she came back with me and we kept her and I began to worm out of her what was really worrying her was the fact that she thought that they would have to go back in the summer to the two women who were taking care of them under - they came into this country under the auspices of the Pope's Children, that is to say, that society that brought a lot of children out of those countries that were in difficulty...

Q: Where were their parents?

Mrs. N.: Their parents had to stay. So I began making inquiries and I came to the conclusion I could see why this girl was worried, and Mother Margaret could see, and at that time the oldest sister became 21, and we said, now we can act. We'll simply say, Maria, you take over the guardianship of your sisters. Mother Margaret was taken care of your schooling, and the rest of the time we'll be responsible for you. And so, when this child found she wasn't going back to those people, she was the happiest child I've ever known. They weren't sisters, they were two women down in the South.

Q: Where did they live when they'd finished the school?

Mrs. N.: Well, you see, when Maria graduated she went, she lived in a room and had a position in San Francisco. Then when Magda graduated - as I remember it, Magda went to, took a postgraduate course at Mills College in Arts, and then...

Q: The money came from her father?

Mrs. N.: No, the money didn't come from anybody. These had tobe all scholarships. Magda was going into debt for hers, and I think we gave her that year. Then Margit went to college, you see. They stayed on and went to college at the convent, and when Margit graduated she married this young Colonel's son, Dick Ritchie, and they have a very lovely family, and Dick has done extremely well. They're living in New York now. I was talking to them yesterday, and how they miss San Francisco. Oh, they miss it so. Then...

Q: And Admiral Nimitz gave her away?

Mrs. N.: Yes, we had that wedding for her over on the island, and Chester gave her away. It was a very small wedding, because the girls had not been around too long. But then came Marta, and she had her wedding in the chapel the beautiful St. Dominic's in San Francisco, and he marched her up the aisle and gave her away. And then he gave Magda away just a few years ago, at St. Timians' church over in San Rafael.

Q: This next question you may not want to answer, but isn't it true that over the years as prices went up that a fleet admiral's salary didn't go up?

Mrs. N.: You know, this may amaze you, but neither Chester nor I have ever been interested in money. So long as we had enough to pay our bills and see our children through college, we never cared a darn, and so the fleet admiral's - no, it never went up, but we never thought that we were being troubled in any way. We had plenty of money. But we did not entertain very much. I had very few clothes. I mean to say, I didn't have dozens of evening gowns when he was CNO or - it was the war, we'd gone there at the end of the war. We were horrified when we got to Washington and found how people were living. And, do you know, we limited our stewards when we did have dinners, and we'd have the dinners that we were supposed to have, we would limit our stewards, you have to serve only three courses and the main course has to be something that cannot be shipped to other countries. In other words, when - they need the beef, they need the lamb, they need these things. You make your main course of something else, and he would have it of lobster or in some way - and I can't tell you how many people in Washington from other countries came to us and said, "Thank you, you are making it so much easier for us. We can't afford to give the dinners that the people are giving in Washington, and when you do this, you make it so much simpler for us. Now, we can do it." We used to ask them quite frequently, "Do you want an official dinner, or would you rather bring your children?" And they'd say, "Oh, let us bring our children. We'd just love to bring our children." And then we would take them to the astronomy - to see the observatory and we'd go and watch the stars.

Q: Do you recall the name of Leonard, a subaltern in the Canadian Army, who was Nancy's friend? A young officer in the Canadian Army who was Nancy's friend?

Mrs. N.: Yes, Leonard - oh, yes, she was talking of him the other day. I can't tell you his name though.

Q: I'll ask her some time. What was your connection with Ralph Bunche?

Mrs. N.: Wonderful. He was at the United Nations with Chester, and the Bunches and ourselves were very close friends. They'd come to visit us. Chester had tremendous admiration for Ralph Bunche, and I think few people in this country realize what a terrible thing it would have been when that Swedish prince was killed if Ralph Bunche hadn't had the guts to take command right away and handle the situation. Chester always said people don't realize how wonderful it was that they had a man there that could do that. And Ralph Bunche is still a tower of strength. He and Chester were put together to get money for the little school ~~there~~ at United Nations, and they got money for the little school, all right. I think Chester tackled some of the oil men down in Texas and got some money. But Bunche and Chester always worked very closely together and been very fond of each other.

Q: Who is Walter Haas?

Mrs. N.: He is a very fine man here in San Francisco. His family is a very fine family. He married Elise Strauss, I think her name was.

Q: How do you spell his name?

Mrs. N.: H-a-a-s.

Q: That's what I had here. I wasn't sure.

Mrs. N.: And his son Walter is the head of Levi Strauss, the Levi men - you know those things, "levis"?

Q: Yes.

Mrs. N.: But they have done a great deal. For instance, there's a building just being given to Mills College, a big pavilion named the Walter Haas Pavilion. He's one of the regents at Mills College. His mother-in-law, Rosalie Stern, was one of the most beautiful women I've ever laid my eyes on. Absolutely beautiful, and, boy, they have been so magnificent in the things they have done in this - for everybody here. I mean to say, the big things they have done. Mrs. Stern had given Stern Grove out here in San Francisco, and every summer they put on the most magnificent concerts there, free to everybody that comes, and people come and bring their lunches, bring their children, and sit there on the turf. There are always a lot of seats, but...

Q: You've mentioned Mrs. Stern before. What was her married name? Mrs. - her husband's name?

Mrs. N.: She was Mrs. Stern. Mrs. Rosalie Stern.

Q: What was her husband's name?

Mrs. N.: That was her husband's name.

Q: I mean, you called her somewhere...

Mrs. N.: I called her Strauss.

Q: I'll call her Mrs. the first name of her husband.

Mrs. N.: I don't know what her husband's first name was.

Q: I think you have, and I'm trying to get these names you've mentioned in other...

Mrs. N.: I don't think I ever knew what her husband's first name was. It may be Levi Strauss, but that's the name of the concern. I think perhaps it was. Perhaps his name was Levi.

Q: Tell me more about Henry Grady.

Mrs. N.: Henry Grady? When we met him, he was head of the Commerce School over at the University. He became Ambassador to Iran, Ambassador to India, Ambassador to Greece. He was a great friend of ours. We were all great friends. This group of us were together a great deal. Mrs. Stern, Elise and Walter Haas, Stanley and - oh, what is her name - Esther Powell, and the Gradys, and we always celebrated Mrs. Stern's birthday, and we always celebrated Chester's birthday.

Q: Now, you've given a description of the celebrations in other interviews. When did the Norma Day incident occur?

Mrs. N.: Norma Day wrote him letters. Now, those letters must be in the Navy Department.

Q: They probably are. I haven't gone through them all yet.

Mrs. N.: She wrote him during the war and she's the one that said, "It is a pity you are not here today because Mother had gotten ready for the thrasher crew, and it is raining and they can't work," and she named the numbers of cakes and marvelous pies and roasts that they had ready, waiting for these men, and Chester wrote back to her and from then on they had carried on this conversation all through the war, and he went to meet her, you see, out there, and I had a letter from her...

Q: Do you recall when it was that he met her out there? What year?

Mrs. N.: It was while we were at the United Nations, so it was somewhere around '50, '51.

Q: Now, what important things, in your mind, the outstandingly

EBP - Mrs. Nimitz - 57

important things, that happened to Admiral Nimitz between his UN duty and his death? What events seem to you most important that occurred in those years?

Mrs. N.: Well, we went to Europe to visit our son. Our son was in NATO in London and he lived outside London, close to Windsor Castle, at Wentworth. We went there and then, from there, we went over to France and Italy for a short time, and then on to the Island of Malta to visit Jimmie Fife, and there he met - we spent seven days practically breakfast, lunching, and dining at the same parties that the Mountbattens were at. The Mountbattens gave a very beautiful dinner for us. They met us when we flew in that afternoon, they saw us off when we left before breakfast to come back, and we had a really delightful time. Chester was very restless during those years.

Q: Is there anything to the story that in Italy the people gathered outside his train window?

Mrs. N.: Yes. It was in the train, you see. We were going from Holland - we went from Holland to Duchy, Switzerland, and then from Switzerland we were going down to Rome, and it was when we were on the train to Rome that, apparently, we didn't realize that anybody knew who we were on the train, but the word got out - somebody recognized him on the train, some Italian recognized his face, and we suddenly looked up and I said, "Good God, Chester, what's all this?" And we looked up, and looking into our compartment

EBP - Mrs. Nimitz - 58

the people were standing just packed.

Q: In the corridor?

Mrs. N.: In the corridor of the train. Then I said, there's only one thing for us to do, if we want any peace we're going to have to pull down our curtains.

Q: Let's see. Now, anything else that occurs to you in those years that would be...?

Mrs. N.: Well, of course he was working with the regents then, and enjoying that tremendously. And that took an awful lot of reading.

Q: I imagine.

Mrs. N.: An awful lot of reading. And also the regents all said he was a tower of strength on that Board. In the first place because when one or two regents - they had one or two very fine regents, but they would blow up, and sometimes things would get very tense and they said, and that was the time when Chester, with his quiet....(Tape ended) humor would tell a good story.

Q: Mrs. Nimitz, who were Mickey, Peggy, and Nicky?

Mrs. N.: They were friends of my daughters. Mickey is now - Michael Salkin, the head of the San Francisco Conservatory of Music. Peggy is his wife. As a team they are a noted duet team, playing on one piano, the two of them on one piano. They played in Europe and they played in this country. And Nicky was the - a classmate of Catherine's at college, and

EBP - Mrs. Nimitz - 59

Nicky is a girl.

Q: Is the proper spelling N-i-k-i?

Mrs. N.: N-i-c-k-i, N-i-c-k-y, that's the way it was.

Q: That's the way the typist had it in your...

Mrs. N.: Yes. Nicky.

Q: Mrs. Nimitz, this one you may not want to answer, but if you feel like it, we have to have it from some source, and that's the last days of the Admiral.

Mrs. N.: He was unconscious for a number of days, but also for some little while - some few days - before he lost consciousness, the Admiral didn't want people around. He didn't want to have to talk, and so I didn't let anyone see him. When he could get up, we would have - we would breakfast together in the little upstairs sunroom, and, of course, we had on our staff one named B. L. Estebal, who had trained as a corpsman but couldn't go on because he couldn't do chemistry. So he couldn't go on as a corpsman, so he became a mess boy. He was one of the loveliest characters you can imagine, and he was just devotion itself to the Admiral.

Q: A Filipino?

Mrs. N.: Yes. Just devotion, and he'd had enough training so that he was invaluable to the Admiral, and it was such pleasure to the Admiral to sit in this sunroom upstairs after the hospital where the food had to be brought from about four buildings away.

Q: This was in the back of the house?

Mrs. N.: He had the room right over the front door, and...

Q: Yes, the upstairs porch was outside it.

Mrs. N.: Yes, over the upstairs porch. Then there was another room next to that which he used as a dressing room, and next to that was the sun porch, and Estebal would take him out there and then they would bring his - our - meals up there and we used the beautiful china that was given to us by the National Geographic - the five-star china. And he had everything the way he wanted, and Estebal could somehow get food into him when others couldn't. Estebal would say, "Just one more mouthful, Admiral, just one more mouthful," and then he would sit there until he was a little tired. Estebal would have given him his bath before he had his breakfast, and then he would go back to bed, and he spent most of the time there. The last few days of his life he was unconscious as far - he couldn't talk or anything like that - and I knew that the last thing that strong man wanted was to have anyone see him in that state. He didn't want it. And there was nobody that was very close to him around here. Nancy would come up whenever we got any danger signal. She would fly up immediately, and Mary would come over from the convent, but the last day or so of his life, he knew nobody and, at the very end, Nancy was there and Catherine was there. Catherine had just come out...

Q: And he was in his home?

Mrs. N.: Yes, he was in his home. My son when he saw him out at the hospital in November, I guess it was or October, said, "Mother, take him home. He's not going to live. Take him home." So I insisted that he be allowed to come home, and he was happier at home and he got on better for a while, he could walk, but these little tiny strokes would come and after those things got worse.

Q: Do you feel there's any connection between his operation and the strokes?

Mrs. N.: No, because he'd had the strokes before.

Q: I see.

Mrs. N.: No, I think the one chance of Chester's living with any comfort was that operation, and he knew it, and Dr. Clark said, "I will not operate unless you agree to it - unless you think I should," and he said, "If I find the condition that I'm afraid I'm going to find, then I would have to operate because there's no spinal fluid going through at all." So he did operate and Chester came out of it, and the first thing he said to Dr. Clark as he came to was, "You know, Dr., I was supposed to cut the cake for the Marines tonight and instead of that you've been cutting on me." And Dr. Clark was so pleased because he thought, well, he's coming out of this beautifully. But Chester had a tendency to pneumonia. He'd always had one, and after getting on quite well for two days this started up. Then he began having these small strokes again, some of which he'd had before. He'd had two or three of them before in past years and gotten over them, and I realized that the kindest thing that could happen was for him not to come out of this because he would never have been strong and he would have been the most unhappy human being in the world.

Q: And he died in the little central room on the second floor.

Mrs. N.: He died in the second room, and it just happened that I had gone in there about 5 o'clock in the afternoon. They had a hospital corpsman on that I didn't know, so I was always checking on them, and I went in and I said, "You've got blankets on him," because there had been no blankets on him because he had so much fever, and he said, "Yes, he's shivering." And I looked at him and I said, "He's not shivering, he's dying. You call and get the doctor right away." And I put my hand on the Admiral and the minute I put my hand on him he stopped shaking, and I leaned over and kissed him while this man was out of the room, and he said, "Oh, I can't get them because someone's on the phone." Catherine was talking to her brother in New York. He said he would come out any time we needed him. And I called to Catherine and said, "Get off the phone." She got off instantly and he got the doctor, and he was dead by the time the doctor got there, and the doctors had all told me this was just a matter of minutes. And I had said to them, when the time comes that you know he can't get well, don't go on with all these ghastly things...

Q: No, such as MacArthur went through.

EBP - Mrs. Nimitz - 63

Mrs. N.: Yes. I said, "Don't go on with all these ghastly things. Let him die decently." And they came to me the day before and said, "We're taking away some things."

Q: Now, you and Nancy and the corpsman and ...

Mrs. N.: No, I was the only one in the room with him when he died.

Q: Let me see who was in the house now.

Mrs. N.: Well, the ones in the house were Catherine and her son, because they were on their way down to CalTec to see whether he wanted to go to CalTec, you see. So he was the only grandchild at the funeral, and he walked with his uncle, and the next day Mary came over and Chester flew out.

Q: Was Nancy in the house at the time her father died?

Mrs. N.: Yes, Nancy was there. Nancy and Catherine.

Q: Now, will you tell me something about the funeral?

Mrs. N.: Well, the funeral. Chester had gone through Halsey's funeral. He'd gone through King's funeral, and they'd written him out and said, how do you want your funeral to go on? And Chester said, "How do I want my funeral? They say I'm due for a state funeral." I said, "Do you want a state funeral?" and he said, "No." I said, "Tell them so." And he did not want to be buried in Arlington. He did not love Washington and he loved it out here, and all of his men from the Pacific were out here. So he said he wanted to be buried out here. The funeral was very short. My son arranged everything. I did nothing about it, and he had his father's - what his father wanted. And so he said all the people that come out that want to talk to my mother, want to say something to my mother must say it before the funeral. In other words, we'll all go over to the club annex to the place on Treasure Island, and my mother and my family will be there, and you can all greet her then, but, he said, after the funeral no one is to speak to her. She is to be allowed to go home quietly. And so I met all of the different people when there was - people from every - there was one thing at the funeral which - it was more or less by invitation only, you see, but there was one person there that just was - there was a hilarious spot to it, inasmuch as a punch drunk sailor who had been in the Pacific Fleet and who came dressed as a cowboy and just - he just was having - he - this was his commander, he was going to be there come hell or high water, and everybody was very nice to him, and Mary talked to him for a while. She said just very fond of the Admiral and trying to do honor to the Admiral, he'd worn his best boots and his cowboy and he was there. The nuns came over from the convent, not to the grave where we had the service, but they came to the chapel and...

Q: It was the chapel here on the island?

Mrs. N.: On Treasure Island. It's a beautiful chapel there, just a lovely chapel, and I had gone to church almost every single Sunday while I was on the island...

Q: How long had you known Chaplain Kelly?

Mrs. N.: Never known him. No, had Plank been in the country, I would have had Plank do the service, for the simple reason that Plank knew the Admiral, he'd been up there to the house, and he used to love the Admiral's stories. Plank would just nearly burst laughing over some of his stories, and I'd had the chaplains up several times, and I would probably have asked Plank, but I thought it was a very wise thing my son had the senior chaplain in the Navy do it, and he did a very lovely job. Then when I discovered that Cardinal Spellman had come all the way out, I said, "Chester, ask Chaplain Kelly to please include the Cardinal Spellman in the service." So Cardinal Spellman made a very sweet prayer over the grave, and he was with Captain Kelly whom he knew very well. So that it was a very simple service at the grave and - as a matter of fact, I realized most of Chester's classmates were going to be there, were just tottering. They were going to be on canes and everything else, and then Admiral Spruance came up for that from a bed of 'flu and they were worried to death about him, so it was a very good thing that it was a very short service.

Q: You know there was a service in Washington?

Mrs. N.: Yes, I know there was, a very nice service in Washington.

Q: Where is the Golden Gate Cemetery?

Mrs. N.: It's between here - well, it's out at San Bruno, which is just down the line a little way, and it's quite different from Arlington. You do not - every gravestone in that place is exactly alike, and they just have the name of the person, birth and death, and of course they did have - Chester's has the five little stars on it.

Q: Admiral Lockwood is buried nearby, isn't he?

Mrs. N.: Chester - when they asked Chester to pick his place some years before, they said, "Now, Admiral, there are three graves in that - there are six graves in that plot. One for you and one for your wife. Now, he said, who do you want in that place with you?" So Chester said, "I'd like to have Spruance and Lockwood." And Spruance took to the thing like duck to water, he said, yes, I'd much rather be buried here than in the East. And, then, when Lockwood died, the other grave went to him, and we'd been great friends with the Lockwoods through the years.

Q: And Admiral Spruance is buried there?

Mrs. N.: Admiral Spruance is buried next to Chester, there's just space for me in between. I remember when - at Admiral Spruance's funeral, I turned to one of the Admirals that was there and I said - er, right in the next grave - the next block beyond - is Kelly Turner and his wife, and I said, "Boy, there are four old sea dogs here that are going to have a conversation tonight, catching up on all the latest news."

EBP - Mrs. Nimitz - 67

Q: Well, I've asked you all my 51 questions...

Mrs. N.: Good, good. Now...

Q: Is there anything you'd like to add?

Mrs. N.: No. I was thinking last night of something that I thought...The Admiral's life at the University meant a great deal to him. He was very fond of the University of California. He loved it when he was out here for those three years, and he was terrifically happy because he talked to all these different men that were tops in their professions, and he was - even one of the aeronautical engineers used to turn his classes over to Chester when he left, not that Chester could teach the aeronautical class, but he could tell these men so much that they had to know about other things, and the classes enjoyed him tremendously.

Q: This is an entirely different question, but it occurs and I meant to ask it earlier. Have you any information about Admiral Nimitz's father, the young Chester Bernard Nimitz?

Mrs. N.: Catherine has a letter which is on file...

Q: I'll see it, then.

Mrs. N.: You will see it. It is the only thing we know about him. Apparently nobody ever talked to Chester about his father, and the only thing we know is a letter which arrived when we were living out here in Long View from a man, I think his name was Lonergan, if I'm not mistaken, who had gone up the trail with his father with the cattle, up to Nebraska, and he said - he spoke - apparently Chester gets a great deal of his lovely disposition from his father, and his father was a very energetic person with this weakness that he had, you see, because this certainly isn't an easy trail, to go all the way from Texas to Nebraska herding cattle. And this man wrote a very interesting letter, and Catherine read it into her script, so that they would have it there. That is the only information we know, and - you see, there were eleven in that family, I think.

Q: I believe so.

Mrs. N.: Yes- Chester was fond of his two cousins that were near his age. One was - can't think of either of their names at this moment, but I know both of them. I think they're - I don't know, one of them I think is gone now, I'm not sure. But he had an experience with one of them when they had some rockets - 4th of July rockets - and they were both very young. Somebody'd given them some rockets to go off that night. They decided to see if they could put one off in a bedroom in the hotel - you have that. So that was quite...

Q: The only place I have that is in Sister Mary's book, I mean Sister Joan's book.

Mrs. N.: Yes. Well, anyway, he said that as this thing started going round the room, up and over, and under the bed and everything, he said he and this cousin were up under the very head of the bed, just praying that it wouldn't hit 'em.

And it didn't. He said he learned about - he learned then the lesson that he used many times later in life, not to meddle with what you don't know how to handle.

Q: Well, Mrs. Nimitz, with the two or three interviews that you've given, together with those you gave with Sister Mary and Miss Nancy, and with the questions I've asked today, I think I have as much information from you as I could possibly desire.

Mrs. N.: I think that - I think his life out here - we had a tremendously wonderful time with our civilian friends. Also, we didn't see as much of the Navy, but we saw a tremendous amount of all our civilian friends, especially the University friends.

Q: Oh, yes.

Mrs. N.: And, of course, the one person who I would love to have had you interview was Bob Sproul, but Bob Sproul, unfortunately, is no longer where you can interview him. I mean to say he's not well any more, and Ida Sproul, his wife, and I are very, very close. I think she's probably the person I'm closest to outside my own family, and she is - her birthday and mine are the same.

Q: Shall I turn this off now?

Mrs. N. All right, yes.

INDEX

for an interview

with

MRS. CHESTER W. NIMITZ BY E. B. POTTER

Anderson, CAPT E. Robert, 28

Anderson, Admiral Thomas C., 31

Aquinas, Sister Mary (Nimitz) 10-13, 24-26, 49, 60, 63-64

Augusta, 9, 12

Austin, Texas, 40

Bailey, Sir Lewis, 7

Batha girls, 49-52

Bloch, Admiral Claude C., 29-30

Brian, Captain and Mrs. Paddy, 14

Bunche, Ralph, 53-54

California, University of, 44

Canaga, Captain and Mrs. Bruce, 14, 48-49

Chicago, 6-7

China, 10-11

Churchill, Winston, 31-32

Clark, Dr. Gale, 61

Day, Norma, 56

Edwards, Admiral Richard Stanislaus, 39-40, 43

Estebal, B. L., 59

Fife, Admiral James, 57

Forrestal, Secretary James, 36, 38

Fredericksburg, Texas, 40-41

Freeman family, 28-29

Funeral, 63-64

Golden Gate Cemetery, 65

Gorman, Mrs., 16-17

Grady, Henry, 55-56

Griller, Family and Quartet, 45-47

Gunther, Admiral and Mrs. Ernest, 28

Haas, Walter and Elise, 54, 56

Halsey, Admiral William Frederick, 63

Jutland, Battle of, 34

Kazanokayama, 12

Kelly, RADM James W., 65

Kerrville, Texas, 1-2, 40-41

King, Admiral Ernest J., 36, 39, 63

Knox, Secretary Frank, 30

Kyushu, 13

Lamar, H. Arthur, 18, 26-27, 41

Lawrence, David, 14

Lay, Mrs. James T. (Catherine Nimitz) 10, 15-16, 24, 30, 33, 60, 62-63

Layton, Edwin T., 35

Lerschner, 14

Lockwood, Admiral Charles Andrews, 66

MacArthur, General Douglas, 62

Manila, 10

Marianas, 32

Matthews, Secretary Francis P., 43-44

Maumee, 5-6

Midway, Battle of, 33-36

Miller, Min, 41

Moore, Miss Susan, 42

Mountbatten, Admiral and Mrs. Viscount Louis, 57

Nagasaki, 13

Naval Academy, 4-5, 10

The New York Times, 48

Nicky, 58-59

Nimitz, Anna Henke, 1-3, 5-6

Nimitz, Catherine (see Lay)

Nimitz, Chester Bernard, 67-68

Nimitz, Chester W., Jr., 63

Nimitz Day, 38-39

Nimitz, Grandfather, 3-5

Nimitz, Joan (Mrs. Chester W., Jr.) 19, 22, 24

Nimitz, Mary (see Aquinas)

Nimitz, Nancy, 8, 10-11, 16-17, 24, 49, 53, 60, 62-63

Pauley, Edwin W., 36-37

Pearl Harbor Day, 18-21; in Washington, 22-27

Pekin, 11

Philippines, 10

Plank, Commander David W., 65

Port Arthur, Texas, 5-7

Pownell, Esther, 56

Pye, Admiral William S., 29

Richardson, Admiral J. O., 30

Rigel, 8-9

Robison, Admiral S. S., 7

Romero Salas, 10

Roosevelt, President F. D., 12, 21, 32

Salkin, Mickey and Peggy, 58

Savo Island, Battle of, 35

Shafroth, Captain John Franklin, 18, 25

Shanghai, 10, 13

Shanhaikwan, 11

Sherman, Admiral Forrest P., 28, 41

Spellman, Cardinal, 65

Sproul, Bob and Ida, 69

Spruance, Admiral Raymond Ames, 32, 66

Stern, Rosalie, 54-56

Stevenson, Governor Coke, 41

Taussig, Joseph K., 7

Theobald, Admiral R. A., 29

Tokyo, 11

Tolan, Mr., 41

Towers, Admiral John Henry, 36-37

Treasure Island, 64

Truk, 32

Truman, Mrs. Harry, 43

Truman, President Harry, 39-40

Tsingtao, 11-12

Turner, Admiral Kelly, 35, 66

United Nations, 53-54, 56

Unzen, 11-13

Warren, Earl, 44

Washington, D. C., 15-22, 37-40, 65

Watt, Morgan, 35

www.ingramcontent.com/pod-product-compliance
Lightning Source LLC
Chambersburg PA
CBHW080613170426
43209CB00007B/1417